The
Judgment
God Desires
to Withhold

All titles in the series
GOOD NEWS IN JOHN 3:16

ALL TITLES AVAILABLE AS PAPERBACK, HARDCOVER,
E-BOOK, AUDIOBOOK AND VIDEO. SEE RUSHWAVE.ORG

The Nature and Character of God

The Judgment God Desires to Withhold

The Blessing God Desires to Bestow

The Eternal Son of God

The Saving Work of Jesus Christ

The Faith God Requires to Save

The Judgment God Desires to Withhold

The nature and basis of eternal punishment in hell

Bert Davidson

RUSHWAVE®
Litchfield, Illinois. United States
rushwave.org

The Judgment God Desires to Withhold
Copyright © 2022 Bert Davidson
Author website: bertdavidson.com

All rights reserved. No part of this book may be used or reproduced in any manner whatsoever without written permission, except in the case of brief quotations in critical articles and reviews. See rushwave.org permissions page.

Published by Rushwave®
Litchfield, Illinois. United States
Publisher website: rushwave.org
Rushwave® and the Rushwave logo ® are registered trademarks

Published 2022. Version 12.03.22

This book is available in multiple formats. See rushwave.org.
ISBN 978-1-62179-005-1 (paperback)
ISBN 978-1-62179-006-8 (hardcover)
ISBN 978-1-62179-007-5 (e-book–EPUB)
ISBN 978-1-62179-008-2 (audio book)
ISBN 978-1-62179-015-0 (video)

Scripture quotations taken from the New American Standard Bible® (NASB). Copyright © 1960, 1962, 1963, 1968, 1971, 1972, 1973, 1975, 1977, 1995 by The Lockman Foundation.
Used by permission. www.Lockman.org

Library of Congress Control Number: 2022950432

Contents

1. The Benefit of Knowing our Own Depravity 11
2. Jesus' Teaching on Life after Death 16
3. The Reality of Man's Accountability to God 21
4. What a Man's Works and Deeds Encompasses 26
5. God's Verdict on Mankind 32
6. Perishing as a Judicial Act of God 36
7. Perishing as being Sentenced to Fiery Torment 39
8. Perishing as being Sentenced to Darkness 43
9. Perishing as being Forsaken by God 47
10. Perishing as a Righteous Act of God 50
11. How a Loving God can Condemn People 53
12. Why Man is Blind to His Moral Condition 55
13. The Holy Law by which God Judges 61
14. How Man Violates God's Law 68
15. Man Violates God's Law in his Heart 75
16. God Judges Man by his Conscience 83
17. Why Good Works warrant God's Judgment 87
18. Good Works cannot Atone for Evil Works 90
19. The Evil Heart from which Evil Deeds Flow 95
20. The Earthly Lives of Those Sentenced to Hell 101

21. The Attitude of those in Hell 115
22. Paul's Treatise on Man's Condemnation 120
23. The Stubbornness of Hell's Captives......................129
24. "Perish" as Used in John 3:16...............................135
    Suggested Reading..139
    Visit Rushwave.org...140

The Judgment God Desires to Withhold

*For God so loved the world,
that He gave His only begotten Son,
that whoever believes in Him
shall not* **perish**, *but have eternal life.*

JOHN 3:16

CHAPTER 1

The Benefit of Knowing our Own Depravity

Understanding the heights of God's love requires knowing the depths of our guilt and condemnation.

The Bible records an encounter between Jesus, an immoral woman (a "sinner"), and a highly educated, religious teacher (a Pharisee named Simon).

> *Now one of the Pharisees [Simon] was requesting Him [Jesus] to dine with him, and He entered the Pharisee's house and reclined at the table. And there was a woman in the city who was a sinner; and when she learned that He was reclining at the table in the Pharisee's house, she brought an alabaster vial of perfume, and standing behind Him at His feet, weeping, she began to wet His feet with her tears, and kept wiping them with the hair of her head, and kissing His feet and anointing them with the perfume. Now when the Pharisee who had invited Him saw this, he said to himself, "If this man were a prophet He would know*

> *who and what sort of person this woman is who is touching Him, that she is a sinner."* LUKE 7:36-39

It is beneficial to contrast these two individuals and their interaction with Jesus. For in them we see a stark difference in attitude — something Jesus Himself will use to relate an important truth.

The immoral woman had a great love, appreciation and affection for Jesus. She not only sought Jesus out with the intent to anoint Him with perfume. When she found him, she could not hold back her expressions of gratitude. Her weeping was heartfelt and sincere, her kisses of His feet were tender and affectionate, and her anointing Him with perfume and wiping His feet with her hair was loving and gentle. And she could not stop doing these things; she just stayed there, continuing to weep and anoint Him. It was as if she could not leave him. This was indeed a very touching and moving scene.

In contrast to the woman, the religious leader (who no doubt knew her immoral reputation) was repulsed by her affectionate displays. In fact, he viewed Jesus allowing Himself to be touched by her a reason to question Jesus' divine credentials. "If this man were a prophet He would know who and what sort of person this woman is."

Sometimes the most outwardly religious are inwardly the most blind.

Jesus, the great Teacher He was, took the opportunity to instruct Simon the Pharisee by telling a story.

> *And Jesus answered him, "Simon, I have something to say to you." And he replied, "Say it, Teacher." "A moneylender had two debtors: one owed five hundred denarii, and the other fifty. When they were unable*

The Benefit of Knowing our Own Depravity

> *to repay, he graciously forgave them both. So which of them will love him more?" Simon answered and said, "I suppose the one whom he forgave more." And He said to him, "You have judged correctly."* LUKE 7:40-43

This is a very simple but profound story. A denarii was a form of currency in Jesus' day, but any form of currency would make the point: there are two debtors, and one owes the moneylender ten times as much as the other.

Jesus allows Simon to arrive at the teachable moment himself. He asks him "So which of them will love him more?" Simon answers "the one whom he forgave more." Jesus then confirms Simon's judgment: "You have judged correctly."

Now it was time for the great Teacher to drive home the lesson.

> *Turning toward the woman, He said to Simon, "Do you see this woman? I entered your house; you gave Me no water for My feet, but she has wet My feet with her tears and wiped them with her hair. You gave Me no kiss; but she, since the time I came in, has not ceased to kiss My feet. You did not anoint My head with oil, but she anointed My feet with perfume. For this reason I say to you, her sins, which are many, have been forgiven, for she loved much; but he who is forgiven little, loves little."* LUKE 7:44-47

In Jesus' response He contrasts the treatment He received from Simon with that of the immoral woman. The things Simon failed to do were likely common courtesies in that culture to visiting guests. Jesus said "you gave Me no water for My feet" — something that would allow one to remove the dirt accumulated while traveling the dusty roads. "You gave me no kiss ... You did not anoint my head with oil." Simon's actions stood in stark contrast to the woman who had wet Jesus' feet with her tears, wiped them with her hair, and anointed Him with oil and perfume.

So what is the lesson? It is as Jesus points out: "he who is forgiven little, loves little." If a person is forgiven a large debt, they will have a greater love, affection and gratitude towards the one who forgave them than another who was forgiven a smaller debt. This is a simple but profound truth.

The sinful woman had an overwhelming sense of her own lostness. She *knew* there was nothing to commend herself to God. She *knew* she was worthy of judgment. She not only knew she was a sinner; she knew she was a *really bad sinner.*

Yet this immoral woman also knew God through Christ had forgiven her, and for this she was deeply thankful. She was keenly aware of all the wrongdoing she had done. Perhaps she was even mindful of the marriages damaged by her immoral acts. But in proportion to her own sense of guilt and lostness, in that same proportion being forgiven birthed a deep love and affection. And to the extent she perceived herself as being condemned and worthy of punishment, to that same extent having her debt canceled caused her heart to overflow with gratitude and appreciation.

It may seem counterintuitive, but the woman's *inner sense of being loved by God* and her *capacity to love God* was directly related to her understanding the *depths of her own wickedness.*

This book series GOOD NEWS IN JOHN 3:16 is about God's message of hope to the world as conveyed in one verse:

> *For God so loved the world, that He gave His only begotten Son, that whoever believes in Him shall not perish, but have eternal life.* JOHN 3:16

This verse can be broken down into six parts which correspond to six core teachings of the Christian Faith. And each core teaching corresponds to a word or words in the verse. In this book THE JUDGMENT GOD DESIRES TO WITHHOLD, we focus on the word "perish," which corresponds to the biblical doctrine of hell. As such, it relates to God's judgment, condemnation, and punishment of sinners in the afterlife. "For God so loved the world … that whoever believes in Him shall not *perish*."

As just shown in the historical account of the woman and Simon the Pharisee, Jesus taught the deeper one's sense of moral debt and sinfulness, the greater his inner sense of being loved and capacity to love God upon being forgiven. So rather than a study of the biblical doctrine of hell and God's judgment being viewed as something negative or merely academic, it should be considered something very positive and practical. For when we understand just how wicked, sinful, and vile we all are; when we grasp just how deserving of judgment, condemnation and punishment we all are; it is then we are in a position to grasp more fully the grace, mercy and love of God conveyed in John 3:16.

> **Contrary to how you may see yourself, your sins have resulted in your owing God an unpayable debt. The degree to which you perceive yourself as guilty, lost and sinful is the same degree to which you will sense God's love for you upon being forgiven. And to that same degree you will also love God, and be appreciative and thankful.**

Chapter 2

Jesus' Teaching on Life after Death

There are only one of two destinies awaiting every person after death: perishing or eternal life.

Understanding God's love requires adopting an eternal perspective and realizing death is not the end of one's existence. Death is but a door to another place. The statement "For God so loved the world ... that whoever believes in him shall not *perish* but have *eternal life*" has eternal realities in view.

The terms "perish" and "eternal life" deal primarily with what occurs after death. Specifically, both have in view a) the time immediately after death, when a man is separated from his physical body and either in hell experiencing torment ("perishing") or in heaven experiencing blessing ("eternal life"), and b) the eternal state, when each man is reunited with his resurrected body to either be cast into a lake of fire ("perishing") or live life on a new earth in God's kingdom where righteousness reigns ("eternal life").

Jesus and His apostles reiterated the idea of these two distinct fates. Note these two utterly opposite realities in their teachings.

Jesus' Teaching on Life after Death

An hour is coming, in which all who are <u>in the tombs</u> will hear His voice, and <u>will come forth</u>; those who did the good deeds to a <u>resurrection of life</u>, those who committed the evil deeds to a <u>resurrection of judgment</u>.
JOHN 5:28-29

And I saw <u>the dead</u>, the great and the small, standing before the throne, and books were opened; and another book was opened, which is the <u>book of life</u>; and <u>the dead</u> were judged from the things which were written in the books, according to their deeds ... And if anyone's name was not found written in the <u>book of life</u>, he was thrown into the <u>lake of fire</u>.
REVELATION 20:12-15

But when the Son of Man comes in His glory, and all the angels with Him, then He will sit on His glorious throne. All the nations will be gathered before Him; and He will separate them from one another, as the shepherd separates the sheep from the goats; and He will put the sheep on His right, and the goats on the left. Then the King will say to those on His right, "Come, you who are blessed of My Father, <u>inherit the kingdom</u> prepared for you from the foundation of the world ..." Then He will also say to those on His left, "Depart from Me, accursed ones, into the <u>eternal fire</u> which has been prepared for the devil and his angels ..." These will go away into <u>eternal punishment</u>, but the righteous into <u>eternal life</u>. MATTHEW 25:31-46

[God] will render to each person according to his deeds: to those who by perseverance in doing good seek for glory and honor and immortality, <u>eternal life</u>; but

> *to those who are selfishly ambitious and do not obey the truth, but obey unrighteousness, <u>wrath and indignation</u>. There will be <u>tribulation and distress</u> for every soul of man who does evil ... but <u>glory and honor and peace</u> to everyone who does good.* ROMANS 2:6-11

> *There shall certainly be a <u>resurrection of both the righteous and the wicked</u>.* ACTS 24:15

The statement "For God so loved the world ... that whoever believes in him shall not *perish* but have *eternal life*" reinforces that only these two eternal realities exist. There is nothing in-between, and this teaching stands in glaring contradiction to other religious and non-religious views of what happens after we die.

Some believe after death we simply cease to exist. They teach there is no longer an awareness of anything — no consciousness of ourselves, our surroundings, or anything else. But this view is completely contrary to Jesus' teachings. The truth is man not only continues to lead a conscious existence after death, but he does so experiencing either torment or joy.

Others hold there is an intermediate state between heaven and hell; a place called purgatory where certain people can be further purified and made acceptable to go to heaven. But again, there is no such basis in Jesus' teaching. There is only perishing or eternal life; there is no in-between.

Some hold our eternal state is not fixed — we may *initially* perish or inherit eternal life after we die, but we can transition from one place to the other. In the afterlife if we perish, we may redeem ourselves and be rewarded with eternal life. Or if in the afterlife we inherit eternal life, we may rebel and end up perishing. But once again, these two destinies are never portrayed as reversible. Once people die not only will they either perish or inherit eternal life, but if they perish they will *never* inherit eternal life, and if they inherit eternal life they will *never* perish.

Some believe after death we are reincarnated; we are reborn to live on earth again either as another human being, an animal, or some other form of life. But Jesus taught the body one possesses in this life, and the soul that is connected to that physical body, are eventually reunited after death. The body with which a man is born is the only body that man will ever know. True, he will one day experience conscious existence apart from that body for a period of time, and his earthly body will decay and become dust. But eventually he will be reunited with his miraculously reassembled, new body, being resurrected to judgment and torment, or to eternal life and blessing.

Another teaching is after we die we become perpetual disembodied spirits. Our bodies decay and we lead a conscious existence, but that existence is void of any physical sensations or dimension. But this teaching denies the physical resurrection of the human body — something fundamental to the Christian faith.

Jesus and His apostles taught a man's soul is inextricably linked to his physical body, and there is a physical resurrection. When a man dies and his body is either buried in the ground or cremated, he exists *temporarily* as a conscious, disembodied spirit. But a day will come when God Himself, with whom nothing is impossible, will resurrect that man's body from the dead. God will reunite that man's spirit with the dust or ashes from his original physical body. And that man will exist in a new resurrected body that will either be cast into a lake of fire, or he will exist on a new earth where righteousness dwells.

The Judgment God Desires to Withhold

The depths of God's love can only be grasped when one understands death is not the end of one's conscious existence. Every person who has died, dies now, or will die either perishes or has eternal life. In John 3:16, the word "perish" has in view the negative scenario of what happens after death, and it is portrayed as the inevitable consequence apart from God's intervention.

> **There are only one of two destinies for you and every single person ever conceived. And that destiny involves what happens after death. There is perishing, or eternal life; torment, or joy; a physical, bodily, resurrection to judgment and condemnation, or a physical, bodily resurrection to life and blessing; hell, or heaven; a lake of fire, or life in a world where righteousness reigns; wrath, indignation, and distress, or glory, honor and peace; living in relationship with God, or living without God. God's love for the world has in view His desire to withhold from you judgment and torment, and instead graciously bestow life and blessing.**

Chapter 3

The Reality of Man's Accountability to God

Everyone will personally answer to the all-knowing, all-powerful God for his works.

Jesus and His apostles taught every man is accountable to God for his works and will be judged accordingly. This judgment will occur after death, involves the totality of all those things done while alive on earth, and serves as the basis of each man's eternal state. The reality of this accountability, and the various aspects of God's judgment associated with it, are repeated over and over again in scripture. Several aspects of this judgment are worthy of note.

God's judgment is according to man's deeds. God examines each man's life, passes a verdict and effects sentencing. Consider the many scriptures that not only affirm the reality of God's judgment, but also teach that man's works form the basis of that judgment.

> *It is appointed for men to die once and <u>after this comes judgment</u>.* HEBREWS 9:27

> *He has fixed a day in which <u>He will judge the world</u> in righteousness.* ACTS 17:31

> *And the <u>dead were judged</u> … <u>according to their deeds</u>. And the sea gave up the <u>dead</u> … and <u>they were judged, according to their deeds</u>.* REVELATION 20:12-13

> *For we must all appear before the judgment seat of Christ, so that each one may be <u>recompensed for his deeds in the body, according to what he has done</u>, whether good or bad.* 2 CORINTHIANS 5:10

> *Every careless word that people speak, <u>they shall give an accounting for it in the day of judgment</u>.* MATTHEW 12:36

> *For the Son of Man is going to come in the glory of His Father with His angels, and will then <u>repay every man according to his deeds</u>.* MATTHEW 16:27

> *The righteous <u>judgment of God, who will render to each person according to his deeds</u>.* ROMANS 2:5-6

God judging every man "according to his deeds" means God simply responds to the evidence presented before Him. If the works are praiseworthy, there will be praise, and if blameworthy, there will be blame. In one sense it is man who determines his own judgment, not God. For it is man who by his works *earns* what is coming to him, and is judged accordingly.

God's judgment is universal. Absolutely no one is exempt from it.

> *He has fixed a day in which He will judge <u>the world</u> in righteousness.* ACTS 17:31

> *And I saw the dead, the <u>great and the small</u>, standing before the throne ... and they were judged, <u>every one of them</u> according to their deeds.* REVELATION 20:12-13

> *For we must <u>all</u> appear before the judgment seat of Christ* 2 CORINTHIANS 5:10.

> *For the Son of Man is going to come ... and will then repay <u>every man</u> according to his deeds.* MATTHEW 16:27

> *The righteous judgment of God, who will render to <u>each person</u> according to his deeds.* ROMANS 2:5-6

These scriptures make it clear every person who has ever lived, is living now, and is yet to live is answerable to God. Their works will be examined by God Himself. There are no exceptions.

God's judgment is rooted in His knowledge of all things.

> *<u>God knows all things</u>.* 1 JOHN 3:20

> *You, Lord, <u>who know the hearts of all men</u>.* ACTS 1:24

> *<u>You know</u> when I sit down and when I rise up; You understand my thought from afar. You scrutinize my path and my lying down, and are intimately acquainted with all my ways. Even before there is a word on my tongue, behold, O Lord, <u>You know it all</u>.* PSALM 139:2-4

When God examines man's works, there is absolutely no misinformation. There are no false witnesses, for He Himself is the witness. There is no misinterpretation of the evidence, for He is infinitely wise and intelligent. There is no failure to understand the context of the situation; He knows the spatial position of every particle in each context. With the infinite, all-knowing, ever-present, eternal God, there is absolutely no possibility of forming an incorrect judgment due to misrepresentation, misinterpretation, or misunderstanding of the evidence. God knows *what* each man has done, *when* he did it, *why* he did it, *how* he did it, and the *circumstances surrounding* his doing it.

God's judgment is just. It is not whimsical, arbitrary or biased. It is completely and utterly fair and righteous.

> *He will judge the world in righteousness.* ACTS 17:31
>
> *Yes, O Lord God, the Almighty, true and righteous are Your judgments.* REVELATION 16:7
>
> *God is the God of gods and the Lord of lords, the great, the mighty, and the awesome God who does not show partiality nor take a bribe. He executes justice.* DEUTERONOMY 10:17–18

God knows all things perfectly, but that knowledge in itself does not necessarily mean the assessment of evidence will be just. Even on a human level, if an earthly judge is presented with accurate evidence but is either biased or prejudiced against the defendant, the verdict and sentence in the trial will not be just. The judge will either show favoritism and forego justice by not imposing the proper penalty, or he will act in prejudice and impose a penalty that is unwarranted or excessive. Therefore to correctly and accurately judge, one must not only have a clear knowledge of the evidence, but also a heart which is pure.

God's judgments are just because He Himself at the core of His being is just and righteous. He therefore not only has a perfect understanding of the evidence, but He also has no bias one way or the other in the examination of that evidence. So when every man stands before God to give an account for his works and deeds, God's judgment of those works will be just, righteous, fair, and perfectly fitting.

> **There is a day where you and every man will stand trial before God. The trial will be according to your works — you will answer for every single thing ever done in your earthly life. The evidence in the trial will be indisputable; absolutely nothing will be overlooked or misrepresented, for the all-knowing, ever-present God will Himself bear witness. And the verdict of the trial will be just; the righteous, holy God will form His verdict without partiality, and it will reflect what is deserved.**

CHAPTER 4

What a Man's Works and Deeds Encompasses

A man's works extend far beyond his physical, outward actions.

Previously it was established that man is accountable to God for his "works" or "deeds." These words are synonymous and refer to anything a person does. But it is exceedingly important to understand what "works" and "deeds" are from God's perspective. Failure to properly understand these terms will result in dismissing entire categories of things God deems as having a moral component. A work or deed, when properly understood from Jesus' perspective, encompasses a whole host of factors.

Works encompass the physical, outward actions a man commits. That God holds men accountable for their outward actions is evident from His prohibitions of specific physical, outward activities. Scripture is replete with activities God specifically forbids and condemns such as idol worship, cursing, murder, stealing, lying, witchcraft, astrology, adultery, premarital sex, homosexuality, lesbianism, incest, drunkenness, brawling, quarreling, disobedience to parents, insubordination towards authority, and many others. God examining a person's works therefore involves His examining the outward activities each person has engaged in.

Works encompass the motives behind each man's physical, outward actions. The moral character of an outward act is related to the motive behind it. Identical actions can spring from different motives, making the same outward action right in one scenario, and wrong in another.

When Jesus was on earth, He would often be asked questions which in themselves were not inappropriate. It was the motive in the one's asking the question that made it wrong. This is why on one occasion when He was asked (by religious leaders!) whether it was proper to pay taxes, He called them "hypocrites," for He knew they had asked the question so they "might trap Him in what He said" (MATTHEW 22:15). The exact same question, if spoken from a sincere heart with a desire to learn, would not have been hypocritical for it would have been born of a sincere desire of wanting to learn.

Works encompass the words a man speaks. In life every man asks questions, expresses opinions, responds to questions, and engages in discussions. He also uses word to teach, correct, advise, and rebuke. He also gives speeches, provides testimony, sings songs, and tells jokes. But God holds each man accountable for all his words as is evident from the frightening message of Christ Himself.

> *But I tell you that <u>every careless word</u> that people speak, <u>they shall give an accounting for it</u> in the day of judgment.* MATTHEW 12:36

The words we speak can bring healing and edify others, but they can also wound, tear down and cause great hurt. "Death and life are in the power of the tongue" (PROVERBS 18:21). We may forget what we said, who we said it to, and how we said it, but God does not. And He holds us accountable for every word that has ever come out of our mouth.

Works encompass things a man did not do. Works can not only be positive, consisting of what one does, but also negative, involving what one did not do in light of certain moral obligations. This is why Jesus stated men would be held accountable when they "*did not*" visit the infirm or help those in need (MATTHEW 25:41-46) and why it is said "to one who knows the right thing to do and *does not do it*, to him it is sin" JAMES 4:17. Therefore a "work" or "deed" not only includes acts of commission, but acts of omission.

Works encompass the thoughts a man conceives or entertains. When God created man, He gave him the incredible ability to think and conceive various types of thoughts. Man can birth ideas, make plans, correlate things, form judgments, and have imaginations. But whatever type of thoughts are in view, from God's perspective they can actually be evil and bring defilement. As such, God holds man accountable for the thoughts he conceives in his heart.

That man is accountable for his thoughts is evident from an exchange Jesus had with religious leaders of his day. They were obsessed with observing certain outward, physical, man-made washings prior to eating. It was not hygiene that was in view with these ceremonial observances; it was moral defilement by sin. In contrast to the religious leaders who held defilement came from not observing these ceremonial washings,

Jesus taught "out of the heart come evil thoughts, murders, adulteries, fornications, thefts, false witness, slanders. These are the things which defile the man; but to eat with unwashed hands does not defile the man" (MATTHEW 15:10–20).

But thoughts are not always conceived in our own minds. Sometimes ideas are voiced by other people, and we embrace them. When we do, we are accountable to God for those thoughts as well.

Works encompass the longings, yearnings and cravings of a man's heart. A man may not outwardly carry out a certain act, but in his heart he may wish he could. He may restrain himself from carrying out his desire for any number of reasons. He may want to avoid a negative consequence such as a fine, imprisonment, dismissal from his job, being perceived as a pervert, or any number of things. But his exercising restraint in no way diminishes the fact that at the core of his being he really wants to act that way.

That God holds man accountable for his evil, greedy desires is evident in a prohibition God Himself sets forth. God's command "Do not covet" has evil desires in view — a yearning to have someone or something one has no right to (EXODUS 20:16).

The dynamics of man's thoughts, desires, motives, intentions and impulses is complex and interrelated. But for our purposes here we must realize from God's perspective the heart has "thoughts and intentions" (HEBREWS 4:12) and "from within, out of the heart of men, proceed the evil thoughts, fornications, thefts, murders, adulteries, deeds of coveting and wickedness, as well as deceit, sensuality, envy, slander, pride and foolishness. All these evil things proceed from within and defile the man" (MARK 7:21-23). Men are therefore accountable to God for the thoughts, desires, and intents of their hearts, even though we ourselves may not completely understand the interplay between them.

When taking into account all these facts, it is clear that works extend far beyond what one physically, outwardly does. A guard may stand motionless for hours while on duty at his post. A tired person may recline in a chair, very much awake but not outwardly moving much. And a quiet person may outwardly appear indifferent to certain activities, refraining from making comments or displaying facial expressions. But in all these cases, from God's perspective everyone is still engaged in numerous works and deeds. There are thoughts originating from within, and other thoughts recalled from others that are embraced. There are yearnings, longings, and desires. There are motives being shaped, plans being made, and judgments being formed. And everyone is thinking, imagining, desiring or fantasizing about *something*. Thus while an outward observer may see a lull in activity, God sees a whole host of things going on for which each will be accountable.

God chronicles all man's works. This is self-evident since God forms His judgment on the basis of our works. God keeps a perfectly accurate, comprehensive record of every single thing a person has ever done. And He does this not just for one person, but for every single person who has lived, is living now, and is yet to live. This is truly absolutely mind boggling, and manifests the vastness of the mind of God.

From infancy though adolescence, and from adulthood into old age, God keeps record of everything. He chronicles every outward action ever committed, every inner thought ever conceived, every word ever spoken, and every yearning ever experienced. Nothing is impossible with God. He knows our works and deeds in perfect detail for "there is no creature hidden from His sight, but all things are open and laid bare to the eyes of Him with whom we have to do" (HEBREWS 4:13).

> **Your life consists of a countless series of moment by moment thoughts, intents, desires, and imaginations. Ideas are birthed, judgments are formed, correlations are made, plans are created, conclusions are reached, and motives are established. These inner workings within your heart and mind usually play out as observable outward actions, while at other times you may keep them concealed. From God's perspective your "deeds" or "works" are comprised of both these inner workings and outer actions. And you will answer to God for everything.**

Chapter 5

God's Verdict on Mankind

God sees all men as hopelessly corrupt and evil.

Since God knows all things, including Himself, He not only knows the works and deeds of every person who has ever lived. He also knows His reaction when presented with all those facts. And in keeping with His infinite knowledge of all things, He has allowed us mortals to hear His authoritative verdict at the trial — we can actually know what the future holds for us. And this is His verdict:

> *There is none righteous, not even one; there is none who understands, there is none who seeks for god; all have turned aside, together they have become useless; there is none who does good, there is not even one. Their throat is an open grave, with their tongues they keep deceiving, the poison of asps is under their lips; whose mouth is full of cursing and bitterness; their feet are swift to shed blood, destruction and misery are in their paths, and the path of peace they have not known. There is no fear of God before their eyes.*
> ROMANS 3:10-18

There are two important observations from these scriptures.

God's verdict is man is unrighteous as manifested by his murderous, destructive ways. Man neither understands nor pursues the things of God for "*there is none who understands, there is none who seeks for God.*" Man does not fulfill the purpose for which he was created because he has "*turned aside*" and thereby "*become useless.*" Just as we are revolted by the stench of a decaying corpse, even so God deems man's mouth "*an open grave*" because of the evil that rises from it. Man practices lying for "*with their tongues they keep deceiving.*" Man's words are exceedingly vicious. Just as venomous snakes spew poison from their mouths, so man spews verbal poison from his for "*the poison of asps is under their lips*" and man's "*mouth is full of cursing and bitterness.*" Man is murderous for "*their feet are swift to shed blood.*" Man is destructive and causes distress for "*destruction and misery are in their paths*" and "*the path of peace they have not known.*" Man has no reverence of God for "*there is no fear of god before their eyes.*"

God's verdict of man's character and works is universal. It applies to all people. "There is *none* righteous, *not even one* … there is *none* who understands … there is *none* who seeks for god … *all* have turned aside … there is *none* who does good, there is *not even one* …" This means when the eternal, all-knowing God examines all people, throughout all time, from the beginning of the world unto its end, the verdict is the same: *no one* is righteous, and there is *not one* good person, *not even one*.

The fact that God sees man as not only depraved, but also universally so, is an exceedingly damning indictment. And it is far different than the estimate man has of himself. Why this difference in perspective exist will be thoroughly explained in subsequent chapters. For now it is important to process the full import of this verdict.

God's verdict applies to men in all periods of time. Typically, modern people and cultures view themselves as more advanced both morally and technologically than those civilizations that existed long ago. But this is man's perspective, not God's. While man has certainly advanced on the technological front, morally he is still depraved. And God's verdict will still hold irrespective of any future scientific breakthroughs purported to revolutionize man and make him a good person. God already knows those advances, and His conclusion is the same.

God's verdict applies to all men irrespective of their temperament. Without question there are degrees of vice when comparing one individual against another, and there is no reason to take God's verdict to mean all men are equally devious or rebellious. But the reality of degrees does not change the verdict. One man may be much more devious than another, but both can still be correctly classified as devious. One man is devious, the other is just *very* devious.

God's verdict applies to all men irrespective of their efforts to change. There are countless "good" decisions men make in the course of their lives, and these are mistakenly deemed as reflective of their core character. We may make a resolution to be a better person, engage in acts of kindness and self-sacrifice towards others, determine to unselfishly give aid to the poor, resolve through sheer will power to stop a destructive habit, embark on various self-help programs to adopt a positive attitude, and participate in therapy sessions to understand root causes and be delivered from destructive behaviors. But all these actions do not change God's verdict: man is universally depraved, and there is not one person who is good.

God's verdict applies to all people no matter how they are grouped. Some deem certain nationalities, ethnic groups, or family lines as morally superior. But from God's perspective there is no difference; all are depraved. There are an infinite number of ways to categorize human beings: by age, language, sex, height, physical strength, intelligence, or anything else. But no matter how they are grouped, God's verdict is the same: all have venomous tongues and murderous hearts.

A verdict is only as reliable as the character and competence of the person giving it. But the verdict heretofore described is from God. And in keeping with His righteous character, it is reliable and truthful. The verdict is not an overstatement or exaggeration; there truly is not one good person who has or will ever live. The verdict is also not born of bias or prejudice; there is nothing in God to distort His judgment. The verdict is perfect, accurate, and conforms to all those perfections that exist within God Himself.

> **From God's perspective you along with all other human beings are murderous, treacherous, useless, and unrighteous. This assessment is true of all people irrespective of age, sex, nationality, ethnic group, family line, or any other conceivable category. No matter how good, honorable, moral, and upright you may perceive yourself or someone else to be, in reality and before God you both are dishonorable and unjust. While there may indeed be a difference in degree of how corrupt you are when compared to someone else, that in no way negates the fact you are both evil.**

CHAPTER 6

Perishing as a Judicial Act of God

Perishing is the result of being sentenced by God Himself on account of the evil deeds committed.

We have seen not only is man accountable to God for all his earthly deeds, but God's verdict on the basis of those works is man is unrighteous, ungodly, unjust, and depraved; there are no exceptions. This verdict necessitates a sentence, for justice must be served.

There is a critical difference between a man exploring a mountainous area and falling into a pit, and his being found guilty of certain criminal offenses and sentenced to live in that pit. The former is a misfortune; the latter is a penal consequence. The one is an accident; the other an act of justice.

The word "perish" used in John 3:16 means to be "destroyed" or "ruined." And the teaching of Jesus and His apostles make it clear what is in view is being "ruined" or "destroyed" in a place called hell. Hell is described using terms such as "penalty," "sentence", "punishment", "repay", "judgment", and "retribution", thereby clearly indicating its judicial character. Consider the many scriptures detailing the end of unrighteous men.

> *These will <u>pay the penalty</u> of eternal destruction.*
> 2 THESSALONIANS 1:9

> *How will you escape the <u>sentence of hell</u>?* MATTHEW 23:33

> *These will go away into <u>eternal punishment</u>.*
> MATTHEW 25:46

> *How much <u>severer punishment</u> do you think he will deserve who has trampled under foot the Son of God*
> HEBREWS 10:29

> *It is only just for God to <u>repay</u> with affliction those who afflict you ... dealing out <u>retribution</u> to those who do not know God.* 2 THESSALONIANS 1:6-8

> *But do you suppose this, O man, ... that you will escape the <u>judgment of God</u>? ... But because of your stubbornness and unrepentant heart you are <u>storing up wrath</u> for yourself in the <u>day of wrath</u> and revelation of the righteous <u>judgment of God</u>, who will render to each person according to his deeds ... to those who are selfishly ambitious and do not obey the truth, but obey unrighteousness, <u>wrath and indignation</u>. There will be tribulation and distress for every soul of man who does evil.* ROMANS 2:3-9

> *The Lord knows how ... to keep the unrighteous <u>under punishment</u> for the <u>day of judgment</u>.* 2 PETER 2:9

> *But by His word the present heavens and earth are being reserved for fire, kept for the <u>day of judgment and destruction of ungodly men</u>.* 2 PETER 3:7

The Judgment God Desires to Withhold

These verses make it clear perishing is a judicial act of God against sinners for their evil works. When we are told "God so loved the world, that He gave His only begotten Son, that whoever believes in Him shall not *perish*," it is stating God loved the world by taking a step to spare man *the judgment God Himself was obligated in justice to impose*. The exact nature of this sentence is revealed in scripture, and will be delineated in upcoming chapters. What is being established here is the judicial character of perishing.

> **Perishing consist of being punished by God on account of the wrongs committed. It is a judicial sentence that flows from a verdict that you and all mankind, without exception, are murderous, deceitful, rebellious, and evil. John 3:16 is stating God's love has been revealed by His taking a step to save you from His judgment — a judgment He Himself as the righteous Judge is obligated in justice to impose.**

Chapter 7

Perishing as being Sentenced to Fiery Torment

Hell's torments can be likened to having one's entire body consumed by fire.

In the teachings of Jesus and His apostles, the imagery of hell is very consistent. It is repeatedly portrayed as a place of torment by fire. Jesus' parable of the evil rich man and Lazarus is a case in point.

Now there was a rich man, and he habitually dressed in purple and fine linen, joyously living in splendor every day. And a poor man named Lazarus was laid at his gate, covered with sores, and longing to be fed with the crumbs which were falling from the rich man's table; besides, even the dogs were coming and licking his sores. Now the poor man died and was carried away by the angels to Abraham's bosom; and the rich man also died and was buried. In Hades [hell] he lifted up his eyes, <u>being in torment</u>, and saw Abraham far away and Lazarus in his bosom. And he cried out and said, "Father Abraham, have

The Judgment God Desires to Withhold

> *mercy on me, and send Lazarus so that he may dip the tip of his finger in water and cool off my tongue, for <u>I am in agony in this flame</u>." But Abraham said, "Child, remember that during your life you received your good things, and likewise Lazarus bad things; but now he is being comforted here, and <u>you are in agony</u>. And besides all this, between us and you there is a great chasm fixed, so that those who wish to come over from here to you will not be able, and that none may cross over from there to us."* LUKE 16:19–26

There is no reason to regard this story as an actual historical account. Jesus is not giving a detailed teaching on hell's environment. And He employs the name "Lazarus" not because he was an actual person, but rather as a literary device — the name means "divine help." Interpreting Jesus' words as an actual story will result in unwarranted questions such as "How big is the chasm? How can everyone fit in Abraham's bosom? So people in hell can talk to people in heaven? And where is the water hole?" Like many of Jesus' teachings, He is telling a story to relate spiritual truths.

One clear teaching of Jesus' parable is the fiery torment of the wicked in the afterlife. We know this because many other scriptures have the same imagery. In the book of Revelation, an angel announces what will be the end of all those who worship the Antichrist.

> *And he will be <u>tormented with fire and brimstone</u>... And the <u>smoke of their torment</u> goes up forever and ever.* REVELATION 14:10-11

In the final judgment, the devil along with those he deceived will be sentenced to fiery torment.

Perishing as being Sentenced to Fiery Torment

> *And the devil who deceived them was thrown into the <u>lake of fire and brimstone</u> ... <u>and they will be tormented</u> day and night forever and ever.*
> REVELATION 20:10

This place of fire, which was "prepared" by God for the devil and his fallen angels, is the same place all evil men go.

> *Then He will also say to those on His left, "Depart from Me, accursed ones, into the <u>eternal fire</u> which has been prepared for the devil and his angels."*
> MATTHEW 25:41

Sinners are compared to weeds gathered in a harvest, or bad fish gathered in a net. Both are useless and burned.

> *So just as the tares are gathered up and <u>burned with fire</u>, so shall it be at the end of the age. The Son of Man will send forth His angels, and they will gather out of His kingdom all stumbling blocks, and those who commit lawlessness, and will throw them into the <u>furnace of fire</u>; in that place there will be weeping and gnashing of teeth.* MATTHEW 13:24-42

> *So it will be at the end of the age; the angels will come forth and take out the wicked from among the righteous, and will throw them into the <u>furnace of fire</u>; in that place there will be weeping and gnashing of teeth.* MATTHEW 13:47-50

Hell is so horrifying, and sin is to be so abhorred, that Jesus exaggerated by saying a man should cut off that part of his body which gives occasion to fall into sin or "stumble." Jesus was not advocating self-mutilation — something that was never taught or practiced by Jesus or any of his followers. But he was indirectly giving a teaching about the need to abhor sin and avoid hell. He repeats himself three times, using a different member of the body: the hand, the foot, and the eye.

> *If your hand causes you to stumble, cut it off; it is better for you to enter life crippled, than, having your two hands, to go <u>into hell, into the unquenchable fire</u>, where their worm does not die, and the <u>fire is not quenched</u>. If your foot causes you to stumble, cut it off; it is better for you to enter life lame, than, having your two feet, to be cast <u>into hell</u>, where their worm does not die, and the <u>fire is not quenched</u>. If your eye causes you to stumble, throw it out; it is better for you to enter the kingdom of God with one eye, than, having two eyes, to be cast <u>into hell</u>, where their worm does not die, and the <u>fire is not quenched</u>.* MARK 9:43-48

In the judgment of sinners in their life after death, the imagery of affliction by fire is used because it parallels the anguish, suffering and torment to which they are subjected. In this earthly life, being burned with fire is among the most exceedingly painful things one can experience. To have just one small part of the body even lightly burned can be agonizing. To have one's entire body heavily burned would be utterly agonizing and is rarely survivable. But it is this latter scenario that is consistently employed in the description of hell.

> **Perishing involves being tormented and afflicted on account of one's evil deeds. This torment can be likened to having one's entire body consumed with intense fire. The sensation of pain is agonizing, unrelenting, and fierce.**

Chapter 8

Perishing as being Sentenced to Darkness

Hell's torments can be likened to being sentenced to the most dark, desolate place imaginable.

In God's righteous judgment, He sentences sinners to what can best be understood as a remote, faraway realm where there is no light. There is only darkness.

> *[They] will be cast out into the <u>outer darkness</u>; in that place there will be weeping and gnashing of teeth.* MATTHEW 8:12

> *Throw him into the <u>outer darkness</u>; in that place there will be weeping and gnashing of teeth.* MATTHEW 22:13

> *For whom the <u>black darkness</u> has been reserved.*
> 2 PETER 2:17

> *For whom the <u>black darkness</u> has been reserved forever.*
> JUDE 13

In this description of punishment, it is not "darkness" to which sinners are sentenced, but "outer darkness." It is as if the word "darkness" does not adequately convey just how bleak, remote and dark this place is. If one could outline an area of darkness, sinners would be "cast" or "thrown" to the outermost ends of that area. It is as if they are thrown into a black hole on the edge of the universe ...

Three aspects of hell are revealed in it being described as a place of darkness: remoteness, desolation and isolation.

Hell's darkness reveals the wicked have an overwhelming sense of being utterly separated. They are remote in the most distant way conceivable.

Darkness can be experienced different ways. There is a difference between being in darkness while in a beautiful, colorful garden as opposed to a deep, bottomless pit. In a garden where there is no light you are still aware you are surrounded by beautiful things. You can still smell the flowers, touch the trees, and feel the wind. And even if you could not smell, touch or feel these things, you would still be *aware* you are in a garden — it just happens to be very dark outside. However in a bottomless pit darkness envelopes you. You are aware the darkness is characteristic of where you are: a place that is far, far away from everything else.

The sense of remoteness and inaccessibility in hell is referenced in Jesus' parable of the evil rich man and Lazarus. Abraham is portrayed as being "far away" from the evil rich man saying "between us and you there is a great chasm fixed, so that those who wish to come over from here to you will not be able, and that none may cross over from there to us" (LUKE 16:23–26). Jesus employs this imagery to reinforce hell is a place where there is a sense of being completely unreachable.

Hell's darkness reveals the wicked are sentenced to a dismal, barren, desolate existence. There is nothing to stimulate or inspire in hell; there is nothing interesting or fascinating. There is only darkness.

Previously the earthly analogy of being in a bottomless pit was used to emphasize the sense of hell being a remote, distant, faraway place. But we can take that analogy even further to emphasize another aspect. A bottomless pit is not only an inaccessible place. *It is a barren, desolate place.*

In our earthly lives God grants the gift of sight and thereby allows us to see the wonders of His creation. There is the peaceful sunset and the blue sky filled with white, puffy clouds. There is the meandering stream, the crashing waves of the ocean, and the majestic mountain peaks. Without even considering the other human senses of sound, taste and touch, the ability to see the vast array of colors, motions and scenes within creation instills a sense of awe and wonder.

But in hell, there are no inspiring sights. There is absolutely nothing to arouse awe and wonder — *absolutely nothing*. Instead, there is just an overwhelming sense of emptiness and desolation.

Hell's darkness reveals the wicked are utterly isolated. There are no companions or friends in hell; sinners are completely alone.

We can take the analogy of being in a bottomless pit even further. It is one thing to be in a remote, desolate bottomless pit with friends, but quite another to be there completely alone. The presence of companions would provide some degree of comfort in the darkness. But in hell there are no friends for there is no mercy.

It cannot be overstated how terrible this is. In hell there is no one to converse with. There is no one to hear. There are no expressions of sympathy from others to be heard. There are no consolations of "this won't last forever; you will eventually get out of here." There are no smiling faces to see; no eyes to connect with. There are no reassuring touches or comforting embraces. There is only complete, utter isolation. Whatever sense of loneliness a person feels in this world, it is nothing compared to that of those in hell.

These three aspects of outer darkness are absolutely terrifying when considered individually. How much more terrifying when considered together?

> **Perishing involves being tormented and afflicted on account of one's evil deeds. This torment can be likened to the remoteness, desolation, and isolation one would feel being cast alone into the most unreachable, barren, darkest pit imaginable. The sensation of anguish is deep, intense and overwhelming.**

CHAPTER 9

Perishing as being Forsaken by God

Hell is the absence of the most meaningful relationship there is, and all the graces associated with it.

In this earthly life, man experiences blessings from God despite his rebellious, sinful heart. Jesus said that God "causes His sun to rise on the evil and the good, and sends rain on the righteous and the unrighteous" (MATTHEW 5:45). Sunshine and rain are displays of God's kindness towards those who are His enemies.

In addition to the sun and rain, God also grants another blessing: the joys and pleasures of companionship and relationship. True, many men turn the blessing of friendship towards evil ends by conspiring to do wrong, just as they turn the blessing of receiving food and water from the sun and rain towards evil by strengthening themselves to commit wrongdoing. But neither of these negate the fact that companionship and relationships are displays of God's goodness and mercy.

Reflect for a moment on a personal relationship you have had which brought you great fulfillment. It may have been with a spouse, sibling, parent, child, or friend, and it may have been a past relationship or one that is still ongoing. That relationship is a gift from God and an example of His grace and mercy to you.

As fulfilling as any human relationship can be, nothing can compare with an intimate, personal, loving relationship between man and his Creator. But in hell it is this relationship which is utterly and completely lost, as well as all blessings associated with it. Consider the fearful words of the end of the wicked, which indicate separation from the Lord.

> *These will pay the penalty of eternal destruction, <u>away from the presence of the Lord and from the glory of His power.</u>* 2 THESSALONIANS 1:9

> *I will declare to them, "I never knew you; <u>depart from Me</u>, you who practice lawlessness."* MATTHEW 7:23

> *Then He will also say to those on His left, "<u>Depart from Me</u>, accursed ones, into the eternal fire."* MATTHEW 25:41

In this series GOOD NEWS IN JOHN 3:16, book 4 is about THE ETERNAL SON OF GOD. There we shall see Jesus Himself is the One making the declaration "Depart from Me." In hell, not only is there no relationship with God through Jesus Christ, but there are no blessings man presently enjoys on this earth. There is only complete and utter desolation and abandonment. The wicked person is conscious of the fact he is being punished, experiencing fiery torment, in utter darkness of what can be thought of as a black hole on the edge of the universe, with full knowledge he has been forsaken.

The absolute horror of being forsaken by God cannot be overstated. Again, there are countless pleasant sensations and feelings we experience in this life which are acts of kindness and grace from God. There is the inspiring sight of a sunset; the soft sensation of a cool breeze; the pleasant variety of tastes when eating; the pleasing aromas of perfumes, flowers and trees; and the sounds of the birds chirping or the rain spattering. There is the sense of refreshment when having a cool drink, and the feeling of satisfaction after having eaten a solid meal. There is the joy of companionship when spending time with friends or family, and the pleasantness of a warm smile and encouraging word. But all such graces are absent in hell. Those common, everyday blessings from God that men took for granted in this life are completely withheld. There is only suffering, pain, rejection, condemnation, and abandonment.

In Jesus' parable of the evil rich man and Lazarus, the rich man "cried out and said, 'Father Abraham, have mercy on me, and send Lazarus so that he may dip the tip of his finger in water and cool off my tongue, for I am in agony in this flame'" (LUKE 16:19–24). But no mercy was shown, not even so much as a drop of water. This is another truth taught in that parable: hell is the absence of all God's graces and mercies.

Mercy comes from God. If *God* says to a man "Depart from *Me*," that man is necessarily cut off from Him who is Mercy.

> **Perishing involves being utterly abandoned by God Himself. The sinner is in no way a recipient of any form of God's compassion and lovingkindness. All mercy and grace that God granted in earthly life is withheld.**

Chapter 10

Perishing as a Righteous Act of God

Man being sentenced to hell is in keeping with the moral perfections of God.

The torments of hell, and the corresponding weeping and gnashing of teeth resulting from it, are without question absolutely and utterly terrifying. But these torments must be viewed through the biblical grid of the nature and character of God. Several points are worthy of note.

The torments of hell are not excessive. It is not that man's works warrant only a minor, passing penalty, and God is simply effecting a harsh sentence because He is unreasonable, austere, or worst yet, cruel or sadistic. On the contrary, God is "compassionate and gracious, slow to anger, and abounding in lovingkindness and truth" (Exodus 34:6). But He is also just and holy. As such, He is constrained by His own righteous nature to mete out justice. Man being sentenced to hell does not reflect God's cruelty, but rather how heinous, abhorrent, and wicked are man's works.

Perishing as a Righteous Act of God

The torments of hell are not deficient. If in the examination of man's works God were *not* to sentence man to hell, He would be negligent in executing justice. Again, God is loving, compassionate, and gracious. But it is also true that "all His ways are just … righteous and upright is He" (DEUTERONOMY 32:4). As such, just as His righteous nature *restrains* Him from executing too *harsh* a sentence, even so that same righteous nature *compels* Him to impose a *proper* sentence. He *must* subject sinners to a sentence consistent with what they *earned*.

God's judgment is reciprocal. There is usually some parallel between the offense and the judgment He effects. This is in keeping with God's righteous judgment. There are several instances where this pattern of reciprocity is seen in God's judgment of earthly sins.

- When king Jeroboam stretched out his hand to unjustly seize a man of God, that same hand was withered (1 KINGS 13:4).

- Prior to the coming of the Lord when the world is engaged in the bloody persecution of God's people, God himself engages in the bloody destruction of those same people. At that time an angel declares:

   Righteous are You, who are and who were, O Holy One … , because You judged these things; for <u>they poured out the blood of saints</u> and prophets, and <u>You have given them blood to drink</u>. They deserve it.
   REVELATION 16:5–6.

- When the Israelites murmured against God after having spied out the promised land for forty days, God judged them and said:

  <u>According to the number of days</u> which you spied out the land, forty days, <u>for every day you shall bear your guilt a year</u>, even forty years, and you will know My opposition. NUMBERS 14:28–34

When it comes to God's judgment of man's earthly works, this pattern of reciprocity is seen in God's sentencing men to hell. God's verdict was that all men are morally depraved, murderous, godless people. They lie, cheat, steal, deceive, curse, and grumble. They dishonor, disobey, rebel, assault and demean. In short, they reject God's *moral light*. God therefore condemns them to that which parallels their moral existence: *darkness*. In the same way, we shall see later that people in hell hate God, despise the truth, and want nothing to do with Him. Even so, God in His righteous judgment grants sinners their request. They are forsaken by God, and condemned to existence apart from Him. All His grace and mercies are withheld.

> **God is right to condemn sinners to hell's torments. It is not an excessive penalty, but instead conforms to what man justly deserves for his works. The fiery torment, darkness and abandonment to which sinners are condemned reflects principles of reciprocity in God's judgment.**

CHAPTER 11

How a Loving God can Condemn People

Questioning how God can justly condemn all men reveals our blindness to both man and God's nature.

People generally have no problem with a loving God sending really bad, evil people to hell. For example, take a war criminal or serial killer who was not only guilty of unspeakable acts of cruelty, but also showed no remorse and actually bragged about his heinous crimes. When people are asked what God should do with such sinners, the answer is "Well, if there is a God, He should send them to hell!" In fact, the same people who object to a loving God condemning people tend to deem God unjust if He did *not* send such wicked people to hell!

When people ask "How could a loving God send someone to hell," what they are really asking is "How could a loving God send decent, good people to hell who have never committed heinous acts?" Their question has several underlying assumptions, namely 1) there is a category of offenses and character traits that warrant being condemned to hell and 2) they themselves along with most people do not fall into that category. So the objection is not really about a loving God sending people to hell, but rather His sending people to hell for seemingly petty offenses.

We tend to compare ourselves to others, and in doing so we can look righteous. After all, if the comparison is between a vicious war criminal and we ourselves, then indeed we will look pretty good. But it will be seen this is a false comparison and faulty reasoning. The truth is *all men are more unjust and unrighteous before God than the most cruel, wicked person is before us.*

Understanding how a loving God can justly condemn all men to hell requires a radical realignment of what constitutes good and evil. Instead of asking "How could a loving God condemn people to hell," the question should be "Why do we see ourselves as good, upright people when we are not? What are the dynamics of deception that causes us to be so seriously deceived about our moral condition?"

The importance of answering these questions must not be minimized. As long as we believe we are essentially good people and perceive God is unjust to condemn us to hell, we will never grasp His love. The message of John 3:16 is God's love for the world was manifested by a step He took to save us from judgment. Understanding God's love is predicated on this fact.

> **God verdict that all are unrighteous and deserving of the sentence to perish in hell is grounded in His meting what is justly deserved sinners. The question is therefore not how a loving God can condemn good, innocent people, but rather why we fallen humans are so blind to the wickedness of our deeds.**

CHAPTER 12

Why Man is Blind to His Moral Condition

We misjudge our true character because we judge ourselves by what is right or wrong in our own eyes.

If even the nicest, kindest, gentlest humanitarian is guilty of committing evils that warrant being cast into a lake of fire, why do we not see it that way? Why do we consider many others and we ourselves as good, decent people? Why do we take offense at the idea that God finds our deeds absolutely reprehensible and worthy of damnation? Examining the mindset of one particular man and how he viewed his actions will answer these questions with absolute clarity.

In the history of the world there have been innumerable massacres of innocent people. These horrific acts of barbarity have been perpetrated by different men from all nationalities, languages, social classes, ethnicities, and colors — any group with which we choose to identify has someone in it with a great deal of blood on their hands. The mindset of one particular man involved in such atrocities provides a clear parallel as to why we ourselves are deceived about our moral condition. True, we ourselves may not be guilty of committing heinous crimes like him. But the dynamics of self-deception will become evident as the historical account of his life is examined. Such examination, however, involves traveling down one of the many dark, bloody corridors of human history — the slaughter historically known as the Holocaust, and the works of one military official in the Nazi regime: Adolf Eichmann.

As the Nazis sought to conquer Europe in World War II, Adolf Eichmann was to ensure Jews residing in conquered territories were properly identified and deported to certain areas called ghettos. The penalty for leaving these ghettos was death, and the living conditions were atrocious — thousands died from disease and starvation. The ghettos served as a holding area until the Nazis determined how best to rid Europe of Jews and thereby usher in the Nazi vision of utopia: a Jew-free Europe.

Ultimately the Nazi leadership determined the "Final Solution" to the Jewish "problem" was to simply put the Jews in these ghettos to death, as well as simply kill Jews when conquering new territories. But this required a strategy on how to carry out killing on a mass scale, as well as a strategy to deal with the corpses. Several deceptive and barbaric methods were used.

One killing technique was Jews would be told to enter certain vans with the promise of being transported to another area for resettlement. But the van was actually a specially designed killing machine. Exhaust was directed to the sealed area in the back of the van where the Jews were locked in, and they died from asphyxiation. Another method was to ask ghetto captives to pack and walk to their new resettlement area. But the destination was actually a large trench where they would be murdered in a mass shooting. Another method was to herd Jews onto boxcars to be taken by train to specially designed killing centers. They would be herded into what appeared to be large bath houses, only to be locked in and killed using an insecticide gas. The corpses were then burned in furnaces.

Adolf Eichmann's role in this extermination campaign was to manage logistics, ensuring Jews were efficiently deported to these killing centers. He had personally witnessed the use of the mobile killing vans, the mass shooting by death squads where victims were left in a mass grave, as well as the conditions at an extermination camp.

The scale of grief and terror experienced by those who were victims of this brutality is beyond comprehension not only because of its depth but because of its scope. Over 6 million Jews were murdered in the Holocaust, and at the height of this slaughter as many as 15,000 people may have been murdered per day. If the victims were laid side by side instead of incinerated or buried in a mass grave, you would see nothing but corpses for over 5 miles or 8 kilometers. And that would be just one day …

As chilling and horrific as the previous accounts are, Eichmann's conception of himself in relation to his works was far from negative. During the war while Eichmann was actively involved in managing these deportations; after the war when he was eventually captured; during the trial where he heard from witnesses and himself gave testimony; and even unto the day of his execution, he never gave any indication he believed he himself had done anything wrong — *not once*. He himself and others testified how he found the murders unsettling, but he viewed himself as a soldier obligated to obey orders. Far from considering himself a murderer, he believed he was a good man who was simply discharging those duties entrusted to him. He appeared proud he performed his duties so well, boasting that he was able to manage such logistical challenges with perseverance and efficiency. And he took offense at the idea he had done wrong or he was anything other than an honorable, good person. He considered the portrayal of himself as a murderer an injustice, and to find him guilty of crimes against humanity and against the Jewish people was unfair.

Eichmann was deceived about the true nature of his actions because he judged himself by a false law created in his own mind. While in a Nazi court his actions would be deemed lawful and even praiseworthy, in another court his actions were rightly considered murderous and worthy of condemnation and execution.

As was stated at the outset of this chapter, Adolf Eichmann was just one of many such men in history. The murderous campaigns of others from different times and countries could have been detailed in his place. The individual rationale for these slaughters may have been different — the perpetrators may not have believed they were simply following orders, but instead were righting a wrong, properly dealing with those who opposed their utopian ideas, etc. But the dynamics of deception on the basis of false law is the same.

We ourselves may not be an accomplice in the murder of millions of people, but we also tend to judge ourselves by the standards we establish, and everything plays out exactly the same. We take offense at anyone who suggests our works are worthy of hell. How dare anyone suggest we are anything other than a good, decent, honorable person? Such judgment is unfair, and we stubbornly maintain our innocence.

This principle of living life according to the misguided precepts of our own mind is frequently commented on in scripture. God warned the Israelites:

> *You shall not do at all what we are doing here today, every man <u>doing whatever is right in his own eyes</u>.*
> DEUTERONOMY 12:8

Despite this command, historically the Israelites fell into this pattern.

> *In those days there was no king in Israel; every man <u>did what was right in his own eyes</u>.* JUDGES 17:6

But God's commentary on this manner of living is clear.

> *There is a way which <u>seems right</u> to a man, But its end is the <u>way of death</u>.* PROVERBS 14:12

We are not overwhelmed by the evilness of our deeds because we judge ourselves based on what is right and wrong in our own eyes. But like Eichmann we will one day be brought before a different court. In that day the things we deemed acceptable or even praiseworthy will instead be the source of our condemnation. The works we viewed as noble, just and righteous will instead be revealed for what they really are: dishonorable, unjust and wicked. And the sentence we will receive is death.

This fallen world reinforces our committing evil works by praising us for engaging in them. But what good are the accolades of fallen men if before God those same works arouse His fierce wrath? If we are to rightly judge our actions and character, we must understand what constitutes right and wrong from God's perspective. For the simple truth is this:

before God, we are all as deceived as Adolf Eichmann in regards to our works and moral condition.

> **You may not see your works in this earthly life as warranting God's judgment in hell. You may acknowledge you are not perfect, but completely object to the idea your works are abhorrent and you are an evil person. But this perspective only confirms God's verdict you are morally blind and lost. You do not accept God's verdict because you are guided by the unenlightened standards of your own darkened, hardened heart.**

Chapter 13

The Holy Law by which God Judges

God has revealed His law in the historical account of the Ten Commandments.

One must be careful when traveling to different countries. Laws differ from place to place, and what may be legal in one country may bring a fine, imprisonment, the lash or even death somewhere else …

The universe and all within it is God's, and it is He who establishes what is right and wrong, just and unjust. And He has revealed His Law through the Ten Commandments.

Historically, the Ten Commandments represented a covenant between God and the Israelites thousands of years ago when they were delivered from slavery in Egypt. The commandments were miraculously engraved on stone by God Himself, and the Israelites occupy a unique place in history in that God entrusted this revelation to them. In scripture the Ten Commandments were often referred to as the "Law," even though the term in certain contexts has expanded meanings (all the laws given through Moses, etc.).

The Ten Commandments may be divided into two groups. The first four relay God's law between man and God, and the remaining six God's law between man and his fellow man. The commandments are:

1. You shall have no other gods before Me.
2. You shall not make for yourself an idol.
3. You shall not take the name of the Lord your God in vain.
4. Remember the sabbath day, to keep it holy.
5. Honor your father and your mother.
6. You shall not murder.
7. You shall not commit adultery.
8. You shall not steal.
9. You shall not bear false witness.
10. You shall not covet.

   EXODUS 20:1-17

Since God is the author of the Ten Commandments, it is for Him to define their interpretation, application and use. And He has revealed these things in scripture. Specifically as respects their use, God has revealed several things.

The Ten Commandments reflect standards that universally apply to all men over all time. It is not that they were only relevant to the Israelites long ago. Instead they represent timeless principles of right and wrong against which the atheist, agnostic, Jew, Muslim, Hindu, or Buddhist will be held.

Yes, even the unreached jungle tribesman taught by the local witchdoctor will be held to these holy standards.

While other nations did not have the privilege of this special revelation, they nonetheless are accountable to God for worshiping false gods, idolatry, dishonoring their parents, murder, adultery, bearing false witness, and covetousness. This will be clearly shown when we examine the apostle Paul's treatise on the condemnation of mankind in another chapter.

The Ten Commandments were given for man to understand his own sinfulness. If a man employs the Ten Commandments to justify himself, he has completely missed the point. God's intent was not for man to say "I have never murdered anyone, and I have never committed adultery, so I am in good standing with God." The goal was rather that man would say "I am exceedingly sinful, corrupt and worthy of judgment. My condition is hopeless, and I need to be saved."

Prior to his conversion the apostle Paul was a Pharisee extensively educated in God's Law. He was trained under a renowned teacher named Gamaliel. Paul was an expert in interpreting the Law (or so he thought) and in keeping all the rules and regulations God prescribed under Moses. Paul's perspective of himself was "as to the righteousness which is in the Law, found blameless" (PHILIPPIANS 3:6).

After Paul's conversion, he saw God's true purpose in giving the Law. In several of his letters he comments on this.

When certain false teachers were using God's Law as a means for obtaining a righteous standing before God, Paul pointed out the proper use of the Law was in condemning us.

> *But we know that the Law is good, if one uses it lawfully, realizing the fact that law is not made for*

> *a righteous person, but for those who are lawless and rebellious, for the ungodly and sinners, for the unholy and profane.* TIMOTHY 1:8–9

The Law served to increase man's awareness of his culpability before God, magnifying both the frequency and depth of his transgressions.

> *The Law came in so that the transgression would increase.* ROMANS 5:20

The Law, by increasing man's knowledge and awareness of his own sin, was designed to produce an utter sense of futility so he would look to God in Jesus Christ for salvation.

> *Therefore the Law has become our tutor to lead us to Christ.* GALATIANS 3:24

So the Ten Commandments should in no way be viewed as a means to secure a right standing with God. They rather serve to show we are sinners worthy of judgment and condemnation.

The Ten Commandments are applicable to activities that violate the general intent of the commands. The *letter* of the Law is distinct from the *spirit* of the Law, but both constitute violations. It is a serious mistake to *limit* the Ten Commandments to a strict, literal interpretation.

The seventh commandment is "Do not commit adultery" which obviously means do not have sexual relations with someone who is not your spouse. But in scripture God clearly prohibits and condemns other sexual activities such as rape, incest, premarital sex, homosexuality and lesbianism. These other activities may not violate the *letter* of the seventh commandment which addresses adultery, but they certainly violate the *spirit* of the command in that they constitute sexual activities God likewise condemns and abhors.

The first commandment states "Have no other gods before Me," but the violation of this command goes far beyond simply worshiping a false god. In the historical context of the children of Israel, this commandment would mean do not regard false gods such as those of the idolatrous Canaanites or other peoples. But the command can be violated other ways. If the ruling principle in a man's heart is drugs, alcohol, money, his job, his spouse, his career or anything else, he has in effect made that his god even though he never knelt before an idol. If his decisions are made with a view towards getting those drugs, having that drink, keeping that money, pleasing his spouse, or holding that job even at the expense of *obeying God* — if these are foremost in his heart — his affections and loyalties are misplaced and he has violated the first commandment.

Scripture condemns numerous practices not explicitly prohibited in the Ten Commandments, but they are listed right alongside activities that clearly are prohibited in the Commandments. Consider these scriptures.

> *Now the deeds of the flesh are evident, which are: immorality, impurity, sensuality, idolatry, sorcery, enmities, strife, jealousy, outbursts of anger, disputes, dissensions, factions, envying, drunkenness, carousing, and things like these.* GALATIANS 5:19-21

> *Being filled with all unrighteousness, wickedness, greed, evil; full of envy, murder, strife, deceit, malice; they are gossips, slanderers, haters of God, insolent, arrogant, boastful, inventors of evil, disobedient to*

> *parents, without understanding, untrustworthy, unloving, unmerciful.* ROMANS 1:29-32
>
> *There are six things which the Lord hates, Yes, seven which are an abomination to Him: Haughty eyes, a lying tongue, And hands that shed innocent blood, A heart that devises wicked plans, Feet that run rapidly to evil, A false witness who utters lies, And one who spreads strife among brothers.* PROVERBS 6:16–19
>
> *Law is ... for those who are lawless and rebellious, for the ungodly and sinners, for the unholy and profane, for those who kill their fathers or mothers, for murderers and immoral men and homosexuals and kidnappers and liars and perjurers.* 1 TIMOTHY 1:9-11
>
> *Mankind ... did not repent ... so as not to worship demons, and the idols of gold and of silver and of brass and of stone and of wood ... and they did not repent of their murders nor of their sorceries nor of their immorality nor of their thefts.* REVELATION 9:20-21
>
> *The cowardly and unbelieving and abominable and murderers and immoral persons and sorcerers and idolaters and all liars, their part will be in the lake that burns with fire.* REVELATION 21:8

When considering the Ten Commandments and these scriptures, it is plain that God's standards are far different from this fallen world.

When a man engages in a one-night sexual encounter he is deemed "lucky."

Musical artists perform and are awarded for songs celebrating immorality, violence, and profanity.

Promotions are received by those who through exploitation and oppression increase profits.

God's name is routinely used flippantly, as a curse word, or in an insincere way.

A "good time" involves getting drunk, taking drugs, or committing or observing lewd acts.

For man to rightly understand His moral condition, He must examine Himself not in light of his own standards or the accolades of other fallen men. He must examine himself in light of God's Law as revealed in the Ten Commandments.

> **God judges your works on the basis of moral standards He Himself has established. The Ten Commandments are God's revelation of those standards. They serve not to justify you, but rather to reveal the magnitude of your sin. Violating the spirit of any commandment is to violate that commandment, and be liable before God.**

CHAPTER 14

How Man Violates God's Law

Man continually breaks the Ten Commandments even when they are limited to outward acts.

It is exceedingly important to let God Himself define what constitutes violating the Ten Commandments. He Himself is the author — they originated in His mind. Only He has the authority to define those works that constitute violating His prohibitions. We therefore must let scripture constrain our understanding of the Ten Commandments.

Consider the command "Do not murder." Murder is by definition the unlawful taking of a human life. But what exactly constitutes the *unlawful* taking of a human life from God's perspective? The only way to make such a determination is to search the scriptures. But in scripture God Himself regularly prescribed the execution of certain people, so obviously the command does *not* mean "never under *any* circumstances take the life of another human being." So just as we let scripture define what breaking the commandment does *not* mean, even so we let scripture define what it *does* mean.

The testimony of scripture is the Ten Commandments are violated in the following ways.

1. **You shall have no other gods before Me.**

    DO NOT DENY MY EXISTENCE. I am the almighty, eternal, personal God who created all things. Do not claim I do not exist, or that I am some impersonal, mystical force.

    DO NOT HOLD THAT THERE IS MORE THAN ONE GOD. There is only one God, and I am He.

    DO NOT REGARD THE FALSE GODS OF OTHER RELIGIONS. Do not give attention to the false teachings of My nature, character, and will that are inherent in false religions and movements.

    DO NOT ALLOW ANYTHING TO TAKE THE PLACE OF HONOR AND ALLEGIANCE I AM DUE. Whether it be your spouse, parents, children, family, or friends, do not make pleasing them or maintaining a relationship with them more important than pleasing and maintaining a relationship with Me. Do not make money, fame, a career, a status, a privilege, a pleasure, or even your own life more important than Me.

2. **You shall not make for yourself an idol.**

    DO NOT MAKE ANY PHYSICAL REPRESENTATION OF ME TO WORSHIP. Nothing created by your hand captures My image, nature or character. I am Spirit, and am not mystically present in any man-made object.

    DO NOT REGARD ANY OBJECT IN MY CREATION WORTHY OF WORSHIP. I created the sun, the moon, the stars, and everything on earth, but I exist outside My creation.

Do not regard Me as being comprised of any element or having any form. The heavens and earth cannot contain Me, and I exist in an incomprehensible way you cannot understand.

Do not worship Me in a way I have prohibited. Worship Me in ways I have prescribed, not in ways I have denounced.

3. You shall not take the name of the Lord your God in vain.

Do not falsely swear. Do not invoke My name to attest to something you know is untrue, or to make a vow you have no intent to keep.

Do not frivolously or frequently swear. Do not invoke My name to attest or vow rashly, carelessly, or without deliberation. Let your "Yes" be "Yes" and your "No" "No."

Do not fail to keep a vow you have made to Me. You are to keep your word.

Do not use My name profanely. Do not speak of Me abusively or with contempt.

Do not use My name flippantly or casually. My name is to be spoken reverently, seriously, and thoughtfully.

Do not falsely represent Me. Do not tell others something is My will or plan when it is not.

4. **Remember the sabbath day, to keep it holy.**

   REMEMBER TO ROUTINELY SET ASIDE ONE DAY A WEEK TO ENGAGE IN SPIRITUAL ACTIVITIES. Contemplate spiritual truths, sing worshipful songs, engage in spiritual discussions, encourage one another to obey Me, reflect on the splendor of My creation, and gather together as a community to worship. Set aside a whole day for this purpose.

   REMEMBER TO ROUTINELY SET ONE DAY A WEEK TO REST FROM WORK AND SECULAR PURSUITS. Do not continually give yourselves to the affairs of this life. Take one entire day to rest. The sabbath was made for your sake, not for My sake.

5. **Honor your father and your mother.**

   OBEY YOUR PARENTS. When as a child your parent gives you a direct command regarding chores, curfew, language, or anything else, you are to obey. Do not defy them.

   RESPECT YOUR PARENTS. When you address, interact or respond to your parents, you are to conduct yourself in an honoring manner. You are not to be rude or strike them.

   MAINTAIN A RELATIONSHIP WITH YOUR PARENTS. Do not withhold the affection and communication they are due. Do not become estranged from them.

   CARE FOR YOUR PARENTS. As your parents grow old and increasingly infirm, do not fail to secure their wellbeing.

6. **You shall not murder.**

   Do not with premeditation take the life of another human being when I have not prescribed it. Do not out of greed, personal vengeance, or some other illicit desire kill someone. Vengeance is mine; I will repay.

   Do not commit Euthanasia. Do not end the life of another on the basis of their perceived quality of life. It is not a right I have granted.

   Do not have an Abortion. Do not take the life of the most vulnerable among you — the life of the one whom I Myself have formed in the womb from conception.

   Do not commit Suicide. I determine when your life is to end; it is not your right to make that decision.

7. **You shall not commit adultery.**

   Do not Rape. Do not through intimidation or force engage in sexual relations with another person.

   Do not commit Adultery. Do not engage in consensual sex with a person other than your spouse.

   Do not commit Fornication. Do not engage in consensual sexual relations apart from being married to that person.

   Do not commit Incest. Do not have sexual relations with someone to whom you are closely related.

Do not engage in Homosexuality or Lesbianism. Do not have sexual relations with the same sex.

Do not engage in Bestiality. Do not have sexual relations with an animal.

8. **You shall not steal.**

    Do not commit Burglary. Do not break into a person's home to take something they own.

    Do not fail to return property to its rightful owner. Return anything you have borrowed. And if you have found something, and you know who owns it, return it to the rightful owner. To keep it is a passive form of stealing.

    Do not Swindle. Do not obtain money or property by deceptive means. Do not disguise the defects of an object so as to misrepresent its sale price. Do not make false promises so as to secure a sale. Do not use a false balance and thereby deprive the buyer of the true weight or quantity.

    Do not Extort. Do not obtain money or property by blackmail or intimidation. Do not threaten another person so as to gain their possessions.

9. **You shall not bear false witness.**

    Do not commit Perjury. Do not make false statements in the context of a judicial proceeding.

    Do not make a False Accusation. Do not make a false, damaging statement about another person.

DO NOT GOSSIP. Do not heartily engage in unconstrained conversation that tears down other people.

DO NOT FAIL TO COME FORWARD WITH THE TRUTH. If it is in your power to correct a false testimony, then correct it.

10. You shall not covet.

DO NOT DESIRE TO POSSESS SOMETHING I DO NOT PERMIT YOU TO POSSESS. If something belongs to someone else, you are not to crave to illicitly possess it.

DO NOT DESIRE TO DO SOMETHING I DO NOT PERMIT YOU TO DO. If I have prohibited your doing a particular thing, you are not to crave to do it.

These commandments provide an overview of the standards by which mankind will be judged. When in a previous chapter it was noted God's verdict of mankind is "There is none righteous, not even one ... there is none who does good, there is not even one ... destruction and misery are in their paths," that was primarily based on how man measures up against these commandments.

> **It is for God to define what constitutes a violation of His Ten Commandments — it is not for you to apply your own definitions. Your understanding of His mind must be drawn from the scriptures, which is His word. Examining the scriptures reveals numerous ways you have violated the Ten Commandments, even when those commands are limited to an outward, visible sense.**

Chapter 15

Man Violates God's Law in his Heart

Many are murderers, adulterers and thieves even though they may have never committed such acts.

God characterizes man as those whose "feet are swift to shed blood" (ROMANS 3:15). And without question, such a statement is charging all mankind with being murderers. From a strictly physical standpoint, this statement is certainly untrue. The vast majority of convicted murderers are men, not women. Shall we therefore conclude that women's hearts are not swift to shed blood? Certainly not, for God's verdict applies to mankind as a whole, not just one sex.

When God states man's "feet are swift to shed blood," He is not stating every person on earth has committed the physical act of murder. He is not even saying everyone has plotted to murder someone, but just not carried it out. Have you plotted to murder someone this week, this year, or ever in your whole life? Many will say no. So what does the statement mean? In what way is God's verdict that all are "swift to shed blood" truthful?

God's righteous verdict that "There is none righteous" goes far beyond the outward, visible breaking of the Ten

Commandments. And the specific commandment "Do not murder" extends far beyond the physical act of unlawfully taking another man's life. There is an entire unseen realm outside man's visible acts that God sees with absolute clarity. In that realm, violating His Law is related to the core of man's being: the seat of his thoughts, intents, desires, and emotions. And it is on that basis that He forms His verdicts.

Man is liable for violating the Ten Commandments through a wrong heart attitude. God's Law must not only be considered from its outward standards, but also from the thoughts, motives and desires from which the outward violations spring.

The false religious leaders of Jesus' day put great emphasis on obeying the external aspects of the Law. But Jesus had an entirely different perspective that would have seemed revolutionary. In the Sermon on the Mount He quotes the Law and expands upon it.

> *You have heard that the ancients were told, "You shall not commit murder" and "Whoever commits murder shall be liable to the court." But I say to you that <u>everyone who is angry with his brother shall be guilty</u> before the court; and <u>whoever says to his brother, "You good-for-nothing," shall be guilty</u> before the supreme court; and <u>whoever says, "You fool," shall be guilty</u> enough to go into the fiery hell.* MATTHEW 5:21-22

> *You have heard that it was said, "You shall not commit adultery"; but I say to you that everyone who looks at a woman with lust for her has <u>already committed adultery</u> with her in his heart.* MATTHEW 5:27–28

Jesus addresses the heart attitude behind the outward violations of the Law. He is teaching true righteousness is not merely external; it is internal and related to the heart.

There are many men who over their entire life have never committed physical acts of murder or adultery. But they have time and again cursed their fellow man, been hateful, sneaked a leering glance or viewed pornography in private. As such, they are guilty before God of committing murder and adultery thousands of times. Yes, committing the physical act of murder or adultery is worse than being hateful or lusting. But hate and lust, though not followed though to their natural end, are still evil and warrant God's judgment.

God judges man for the wicked words that reflect his evil heart. Jesus taught that while the core of man's being — his heart — is unseen, the words he speaks flow out of his heart and reveal its nature. He expressed this in His rebuke of the Pharisees who constantly spoke evil of Him. Jesus said:

> *You brood of vipers, how can you, being evil, speak what is good? For <u>the mouth speaks out of that which fills the heart</u>.* MATTHEW 12:34

The Pharisees abiding, unrighteous hatred manifested itself in their vicious, falsely accusatory words against Jesus. It was the natural outworking of who they were. In contrast when Jesus referred to them as snakes, He was not speaking out of hostility or being falsely accusatory. He was speaking the truth.

James addresses the inability of man to control his tongue, and how it defiles mankind.

> *So also the tongue is a small part of the body, and yet it boasts of great things. See how great a forest is set aflame by such a small fire! And <u>the tongue is a fire, the very world of iniquity; the tongue is set among our members as that which defiles the entire body, and sets on fire the course of our life, and is set on fire by hell</u>... no one can tame the tongue; it is a restless evil and full of deadly poison. With it we bless our Lord and Father, and with it we curse men, who have been made in the likeness of God; from the same mouth come both blessing and cursing. My brethren, these things ought not to be this way.* JAMES 3:5–10

Consider the types of vicious words that come out of our mouths. We say things like "I wish you were dead;" "I hate you;" or "I will never forgive you." We also call others derogatory names that are far worse than "good-for-nothing" or "fool." When we make these statements, afterwards we may be filled with remorse and say "I'm sorry; I didn't mean that." But our corrective statement is in one sense true, and in another sense false. In the moment we made the vicious statement, we actually *did* mean it; *that is why we said it*. We spoke from out heart, for out of the heart the mouth speaks. And yes, when we apologized we meant that too; our initial hateful statement may not be an abiding attitude toward the one who offended us. But the fact remains the initial words that came out of our heart were murderous in spirit.

Man has perfected hurling out insults in the entertainment industry. Comedy shows are typically filled with people who do nothing but tear each other down in one way or another. There is nothing wrong with comedy per se. But when it consists of activities that violate the command of God, it ought not be considered humorous.

Jesus said:

> *Every careless word that people speak, they shall give an accounting for it in the day of judgment.*
> MATTHEW 12:36

Man is accountable before God for *everything* he has ever spoken, from his youth into his old age. He will answer for *every single time* he cursed, insulted, mocked, demeaned, belittled, threatened, slandered, or maligned. *When God judges man for his words, He is ultimately judging his heart.*

God judges man for wicked heart attitudes that go unspoken. Our contempt for others is not always traceable to words. How often have we ourselves either engaged in or been subject to "the silent treatment"? In such situations words are never spoken, but there is a coldness, distance, and air of contempt against the one who offended us. We avoid giving or receiving a physical touch, or making eye contact. Other times we are more deceitful and quietly do something we know irritates the offender. Indeed, there are many vicious, vengeful acts we disguise by making them appear either accidental or even caring.

God's characterization of a murderer is very, very clear.

> *Everyone who hates his brother is a murderer.*
> 1 JOHN 3:15

Hatred is an attitude of the heart, so a person can be hateful without ever speaking a word. Hate involves a spirit of ill-will against another person, and it is physical, premeditated murder in seed form. As such, man is held accountable for a heart attitude of contempt.

God judges man for his evil desires. The commandment "You shall not covet" clearly has this in view. It prohibits yearning for something one has no right to possess — the person or thing belongs to someone else. Therefore the desire to take it for oneself is evil.

Coveting often occurs when a thin line is crossed regarding sensations or observations. A hungry person will find the aromas of a cooked meal pleasing. And in the garden of Eden, the tree of knowledge of good and evil was pleasant to look at, even though eating from it was forbidden (GENESIS 2:8-9). And scripture notes certain people, such as Joseph, were very handsome (GENESIS 39:6). These sensations and observations are just human physiology in action. But when these transition to evil yearnings; when the hungry man *yearns* to *steal* the food, when the wife of Joseph's master *desired* to commit *adultery* with Joseph, and when Eve *longed* to *eat* the fruit of the tree, covetousness entered. "Each one is tempted when he is carried away and enticed by his own lust. Then when lust has conceived, it gives birth to sin" (JAMES 1:14-15).

Man's standards are far different than God's as respects covetousness. The world often considers desires morally neutral and says "wanting or craving something is not evil; it's just whether you choose to act on that desire." But this is man's standard, not God's. From God's perspective, when we yearn for something we ought not, *we are sinning*.

God judges man for the evil thoughts he conceives. There is a moral dimension to the conception of a thought. All thoughts are not morally neutral, nor is it that man is liable only when he follows through on a thought. Simply conceiving a thought can be evil.

Jesus cataloged the type of evil thoughts that can come out of man's heart and bring defilement.

> *For from within, out of the heart of men, proceed the evil thoughts, fornications, thefts, murders, adulteries, deeds of coveting and wickedness, as well as deceit, sensuality, envy, slander, pride and foolishness. All these evil things proceed from within and defile the man.* MARK 7:21–23

Consider the implications of Jesus' words. An offended man may conceive the thought to retaliate against his offender with an insult. A married man may see a woman and ponder adulterous thoughts. A thief may see a costly item and consider stealing it. In all these cases, the man may not follow through and act upon his thoughts. He may bounce the idea back and forth, and inwardly deliberate over the pros and cons before actually deciding not to follow through. But from God's perspective, the man has still defiled himself because of what he *thought*.

Evil spirits play a role in evil thoughts. This is not to suggest every evil thought necessarily has as its source an evil spirit. But scripture clearly testifies there is a relationship between the two. Satan put in the heart of men to murder Job's servants and steal his livestock (JOB 1:12-17). The devil put into the heart of Judas Iscariot to betray Jesus (JOHN 13:3). Satan was behind Peter's rebuke of Jesus, and Jesus responded to Peter by rebuking Satan (MATTHEW 16:23). And the devil put it in the heart of Ananias to lie (ACTS 5:3). In all these cases, the parties involved were unaware they were acting on promptings from an evil spirit. But that was in fact the case. They unwittingly were instruments of Satan and fulfilling his will.

Scripture portrays the world as under Satan's dominion. Jesus said he is "the ruler of this world" (JOHN 14:30). And Paul told the Ephesian Christians "our struggle is not against flesh and blood, but against the rulers, against the powers, against the world forces of this darkness, against the spiritual forces of wickedness in the heavenly places" (EPHESIANS 6:12). The realm of Satan's reach is primarily in telling lies, and "whenever he speaks a lie, he speaks from his own nature, for he is a liar and the father of lies" (JOHN 8:44). And in some way that scripture does not fully delineate, the powers of darkness are instrumental in implanting those lies in the hearts and minds of men.

Once again man's standards are far different than God's in the realm of thoughts. The world deems the entrance and consideration of a thought as merely part of the deliberative process with no moral or spiritual dimension. But this is not the case. God not only knows our thoughts; He holds us accountable for our thoughts — especially when they are born of the devil.

> **God not only judges your outward, visible actions. He also judges your inward, unseen heart attitudes. These include evil thoughts you may have conceived, many of which may have been inspired by evil spirits and which you embraced. Your heart attitude also includes sinful yearnings for things God prohibits you to have. Even if you do not follow through with carrying out your evil thoughts and desires, you nonetheless violate the spirit of the Ten Commandments and are liable before God.**

Chapter 16

God Judges Man by his Conscience

When a man violates his own conscience, before God he is guilty of sin.

The Ten Commandments provide standards by which man will be judged. But that Law does not provide a black and white, right and wrong verdict of every possible action in every conceivable situation. Cultures, families and individuals have different convictions on what constitutes violating those standards.

Consider the concept of middle-aged children honoring their elderly parents — something every culture deems appropriate, even those that are unaware that honoring parents is a revealed command of God. In one culture the son may deem it honoring to seat his elderly father at the head of the table; to do anything less would be to show disrespect. Now there is no revealed command of God on table seating arrangements, so strictly speaking, the son could still be honoring his father no matter where he seated him. Nonetheless since in his conscience honoring his father consist of seating him at the head of the table, failing to do so would be to dishonor his father before God.

Man's conscience serves a judicial role by approving or disapproving of his deeds, passing a verdict on whether they are right or wrong. His conscience impels him towards the "right" action, dissuades him from the "wrong" action, and either affirms or condemns him in accordance with the course of action he took. Violating our conscience produces a sense of guilt.

Now God is clear regarding how He judges people as respects their conscience.

God judges man for violating his conscience. James said:

> *Therefore, to one who knows the right thing to do and does not do it, to him it is sin.* JAMES 4:17

To "know" what is "the right thing to do" is the sphere of conscience. And to not follow the dictates of one's conscience is to sin.

How many times have we violated our conscience in our entire life? Is it even possible to count? How many times have we allowed peer pressure, pride, selfishness, or illicit desire quell that still, small voice? We knew we should not do it, but we cast off all restraint. And afterward our heart condemned us, and we carried the burden of guilt.

God judges man for hardening his heart to his conscience. The first time a man violates his conscience in a specific activity, there may be much guilt. But as he continues to violate his conscience and engage in that activity, his heart becomes more and more hardened. He can actually reach the point where his conscience does not bother him at all.

God Judges Man by his Conscience

The apostle Paul considered the natural state of fallen man is one of callousness. And this results in man descending to greater depths of evil.

> *Walk no longer just as the Gentiles also walk, in the futility of their mind, being darkened in their understanding, excluded from the life of God because of the ignorance that is in them, because of the hardness of their heart; <u>and they, having become callous, have given themselves over to sensuality for the practice of every kind of impurity with greediness</u>.*
> EPHESIANS 4:17–19

A callous heart is one that has become dead to feeling; there is no more shame. What previously may have made a man uncomfortable he now rationalizes. As such he gives himself over to practicing evil.

The entertainment industry clearly shows how the conscience can be degraded. Many photos, movie scenes or song lyrics that years ago were considered taboo are now met with indifference or even considered artistic. What previously would have brought a gasp is now met with a yawn or even a cheer. Everyone *anticipates* hearing or seeing more of the same. What has happened to society? The answer is simple: the conscience has been utterly degraded, and so very few things are considered indecent.

How many activities do we now engage in that at one time violated our conscience? If we truthfully examined ourselves, there would likely be many things. But the problem is the very mind with which we self-examine. Since our hearts have become callous even our memory is distorted, and we do not recall how ashamed we use to be. And even when we do recall, we feel no twinge of conscience because we deem ourselves as having matured. But the reality is we have not matured; we have given ourselves over to that which we ought not.

> **God judges you based on how you responded to your conscience. Your conscience serves a judicial role, affirming or condemning actions accordingly. Repeatedly violating your conscience in a specific area leads to callousness and greater indifference to that activity. To violate your conscience is to sin before God.**

CHAPTER 17

Why Good Works warrant God's Judgment

The moral character of a deed is related to the one to whom the deed was performed.

People are certainly capable of acting in unselfish ways by helping the poor, forgiving petty offenses, and even sacrificing their own life for another. Since we consider such acts good and honorable, we may think such works also win favor with God. The opposite, however, is actually true. An illustration will make this clear.

A certain wife would often set the mood for a romantic evening with her husband. She would put on his favorite dress, set her hair, don perfume, and have his favorite meal prepared in an intimate setting. When he came home from work, those evenings were always very special for both of them …

One day the husband had to leave town for a few days. However midway through the week plans changed and he was able to return home, so he decided he would surprise his wife. He quietly entered the front door, and to his surprise he smelled that familiar perfume and saw his favorite meal prepared in that intimate setting. In the distance he also saw his wife in that stunning dress. He thought to himself "How did she know I was coming home?" But as he approached and was about to announce his entry, he was shocked to find another man. She actually was not expecting him, and was committing adultery.

How will the husband respond to his wife's works? Does he take pleasure in her dressing up, setting her hair, donning perfume, or preparing the meal? Of course not. Why? *Because she did those works for another man.* Those works, when done in the context of an illicit relationship, are actually a source of offense and arouse great wrath.

God does not desire us simply to be unselfish, forgive, tell the truth, be kind, help the poor, and so on. He desires us to do these works *as unto Him.* It is possible for people to perform "good" deeds out of reverence to a false god, or with a view towards a humanistic ideal to make the world a better place, or even with a goal to honor their conscience and simply do what they think is the right thing. But since in all these cases the works were done with regard to something other than the true God, then from God's perspective all such works are tantamount to spiritual adultery.

In prior chapters we noted if we are to rightly judge ourselves, we must not only consider outward actions but also our inner thoughts, attitudes, desires and conscience as well. But here we must go even further. Even if in a certain context we adopt an inner heart attitude to forgive, love, show patience, or be generous, those works in and of themselves are not meritorious. A vital component in discerning the true character of our works is considering on whose account our works were rendered.

Why Good Works warrant God's Judgment

The very first commandment of the Ten Commandments is to "have no other gods before Me." But the world creates its own standards and disassociates this commandment from works, and thereby wrongly regards people as "good." There are countless examples of this. A wife may earnestly seek to reconcile with her wayward husband. A wealthy person may have compassion and provide a large donation for some philanthropic cause. A thief may repent and resolve to provide restitution to his victims. A gambling, drunken father may resolve to forsake his ways and become responsible to his family. A conscientious person may engage in numerous acts of heroism to rescue others. To the world, these facts alone make such people "good." But those are the world's standards, not God's. For God, the issue is on whose behalf those deeds were carried out.

> **You are certainly capable of performing unselfish, heroic deeds that from a human perspective are honorable. But those very deeds, when done with a view to please anyone else other than the true God, are actually a source of offense to Him. They constitute a violation of the commandment to "have no other gods," and thereby only add to your judgment.**

CHAPTER 18

Good Works cannot Atone for Evil Works

Neither the quality nor quantity of man's good works acquit him before God.

Consider this illustration. All were silent as the judge prepared to read his verdict. The man before him was a brutal, murderous warlord guilty of heinous crimes against the men, women and children of numerous villages. The prosecution argued for the death penalty, providing incontrovertible evidence of his terrible crimes. The defense argued for his acquittal, providing incontrovertible evidence of his good deeds. The judge made his decision and said:

> The accused is indeed guilty of these crimes. But it must be kept in mind that he did good things too. He did give money to help his poor relatives, and he also provided leadership in the building of a hospital in his community. I therefore judge these good deeds warrant a dismissal of all charges, for these good works atone for all the wrongs he committed.

If the above scenario sounds ridiculous, it is intended to be. Such a verdict would rightly be considered a mockery of justice. But what exactly irks us about the ruling? We can make several observations.

First, the judge spoke of good works which "atone" for the bad works. Atonement is a judicial concept which has in view good works which satisfy the demands of justice and thereby acquit the guilty party.

In the illustration it is not the *concept* of atonement we find revolting for we all accept the concept in one way or another almost every day. When we are personally offended, we believe the offender must do something to make amends. It may involve showing remorse and giving an apology, repairing or paying for the object that what was broken, providing a refund for the damaged goods, and so on. When that action is accomplished, whether we realize it or not we are viewing the offense as having been "atoned" for. We are adopting the perspective he has made amends or provided satisfaction for his offense. So we apply principles of atonement to everyday life and think nothing of it.

If the *concept* of atonement in the judge's ruling is not what we find revolting, then what is it? It is the weights, so to speak, the judge used on the scales of justice. If the warlord's evil deeds were somehow placed on one side of a judicial scale, placing his good deeds on the other side would absolutely not outweigh or even balance his hideous offenses. How does donating money to poor relatives warrant dismissing charges of brutality and murder? It does not. It is therefore the judge's gross *misapplication* of judicial principles of atonement that we find revolting.

Now man takes this whole concept of atonement and often applies it to himself in relation to God. He says to himself,

"I certainly have done things wrong in my life, but I also have done many good things. When I stand before God, those good works will outweigh the bad, and I will not be condemned. Overall I am a good person." But there are major problems with this perspective.

Man viewing his good works as atoning for his evil works is another example of man doing what is right in his own eyes. As has already been shown in a previous chapter, man incorrectly assesses his moral condition because he forms judgments based on what is right or wrong in his own eyes. Thus there are many deeds man considers good but God considers evil. But man not only misperceives the quality of his individual deeds. Man also projects upon God his own warped principles of justice and atonement. In his fallen, corrupted mind he determines the basis of his own acquittal.

What gives man the right to determine what good works makes amends for his evil works before almighty God? Is this not a display of the utmost arrogance and pride? Should a *criminal* stand before a court and say to the judge "I have done good things in my life, so you have no right to condemn me"? Is it for the *criminal* to dictate to a court what the standards of justice should be? If this is true for human courts, is it not even more so for the court of almighty God?

Man's good works before God are detestable and abhorrent, so there is no possibility of atonement. The idea of good works outweighing the bad works presupposes man is actually capable of good works. But scripture disagrees.

> *For all of us have become like one who is unclean,*
> *And all our righteous deeds are like a filthy garment;*

Good Works cannot Atone for Evil Works

> *And all of us wither like a leaf, And our iniquities, like the wind, take us away.* ISAIAH 64:6

The "filthy garment" referenced here is a used menstrual rag, and that is how God sees our good works. "Our *righteous deeds* are like a filthy garment"; they are disgusting and revolting. So the entire concept of God putting our evil works on one side of a scale, and our good deeds on the other, is a complete deception. All our works actually belong on one side of the scale: the side of evil works. There is nothing to put on the other side; there is actually nothing to commend us to God.

The good works God commands of Christians do not atone for their evil works. Without question the New Testament is filled with numerous commands from God for Christians to obey. Getting baptized, partaking of the Lord's Supper, regularly attending church, forgiving fellow believers, loving one another, and helping the needy are just a few. But obeying these commands is never portrayed as a means to secure favor with God and atone for one's sins.

Some make the serious error of viewing the New Testament as an updated rule book — just obey the commands of Jesus and His apostles to love, and your good works will acquit you of any wrongdoing. But this mindset completely misrepresents the spirit in which Christ' commands are to be obeyed. Atonement is achieved through Jesus Christ' sacrifice on the cross, and it is appropriated by faith. Believers are to obey God's commands in response to the grace shown through the sacrifice of His only Son, and out of their love for God. "Beloved, if God so loved us, we also ought to love one another" (1 JOHN 4:11) . And again, "We love, because He first loved us" (1 JOHN 4:19). In this series GOOD NEWS IN

JOHN 3:16, this concept of atonement will be fully explored in book 5 THE SAVING WORK OF JESUS CHRIST.

God alone has the right to determine what is necessary to atone for man's evil works. God alone is all-knowing and ever-present; only He has a complete, infallible record of everything we have ever done. God alone is just and righteous; only He is capable of examining the evidence with complete impartiality. And it is the prerogative of God, and God alone, to determine what is necessary to atone for man's sins. And He has determined there is *absolutely nothing* man can do to acquit himself. Man is incapable of atoning for his evil deeds.

> **It is not for you to project upon God what constitutes acquittal for your evil works. And you have no good works to place on the scales of justice anyway, for your perceived good deeds are actually abhorrent to God. Only God Himself, as the righteous Judge, reserves the right to determine the proper basis of your acquittal. And God has determined your perceived good deeds in no way atone for your evil deeds.**

CHAPTER 19

The Evil Heart from which Evil Deeds Flow

Man is born with a sinful nature that impels him towards rebellion and evil.

We have seen that Jesus viewed all mankind as having violated God's laws and thereby earned judgment. But this only reveals one of man's problems. Even if somehow a person could be forgiven every single one of their prior offenses, they would still commit many of those same evils again and again. This would occur because man's heart is inclined to do evil instead of good.

Paul identified the various attitudes and behaviors that comprise man's fallen nature. He associated them with man's mortal human body, and used the term "flesh" to represent not human nature per se, but man's fallen human nature.

> *Now the deeds of the flesh are evident, which are: immorality, impurity, sensuality, idolatry, sorcery, enmities, strife, jealousy, outbursts of anger, disputes, dissensions, factions, envying, drunkenness, carousing, and things like these, of which I forewarn you,*

The Judgment God Desires to Withhold

> *just as I have forewarned you, that those who practice such things will not inherit the kingdom of God.*
> **Galatians 5:19–21**

When we speak of a creature having a certain *nature*, we mean the *prevailing* or *dominant* tendencies inherent in it. Different creatures are characterized by different sets of behaviors. Squirrels gather nuts, gophers burrow holes, beavers build dams, birds build nests, dogs run on four legs, and lions are predators — these behaviors are instinctive to these creatures. Yes, a circus performer can train a dog to temporarily walk on two legs, and a lion tamer can train a lion not to devour him. But in such cases the nature of these creatures has not been changed, but only *temporarily subdued*.

The world has its own views on the nature of man. Some believe people are born basically good but then become corrupted by either imitating the evil they see or being negatively impacted by various external factors — if we just put people in a good, loving environment, or if we eliminate stumbling blocks such as poverty, everyone will naturally be good. Others believe people are born having no inclination one way or the other and simply adopt the values impressed upon them by their upbringing, society, and so on.

While there certainly is truth in the idea evil is imitated, God's perspective is even apart from witnessing bad examples the entire human race is from birth inclined towards doing wrong. Yes, mankind can do things like forgive, share, and so on. But he tends to gravitate toward acting selfishly, immorally and defiantly as opposed to unselfishly, faithfully and obediently towards God. As such, he has a sinful nature. Man's works and scripture itself testifies to this fact.

Man's sinful nature is testified by merely observing man's works. We do not even need to consult the Bible to know man is corrupt at his core. All we have to do is look at the way he acts.

Man's sinful nature is evident by its universality over time. Without question modern man has advanced from where he was thousands of years ago. But this is only true technologically, not morally. The works of the flesh are just as present today as they were long ago. And this will continue to be the case in the future. Indeed, while man views things such as abortion, living together, and same sex relationships as moral advancements, they actually reflect moral steps backward.

Man's sinful nature is evident by its universality throughout the world. There is not one culture in the entire world that has ever been characterized by righteousness. It is not that if we were to find some unreached people group deep in the heart of the jungle, we would find a loving, caring, godly society. Not at all. Instead we would find tribal wars, selfishness and immorality. There is no such place as Shangri-la.

Man's sinful nature is evident by how he tends towards sin even in his youth. Children can be very selfish — every parent knows this. And defiance and tantrums characterize even toddlers. These activities occur not because the child observed them, but because it is their nature.

Man's sinful nature is evident by the restraint required to contain his evil tendencies. What would happen if parents never corrected, disciplined, or controlled their children? What would happen in a society where all criminal penalties were removed? Absolute chaos would ensue. The reason children and societies maintain a semblance of moral order is due to coercive measures.

Man's sinful nature is evident by his inability to free himself of sinful habits. If a man knows a certain thing is morally wrong and ultimately destructive to himself, why does he not just simply stop doing it? Why does he find himself trapped in patterns of behavior he cannot escape? It is because it is his nature to be that way.

Man's sinful nature is evident by his inability to restrain evil desires. Why do we still yearn to do something we know we ought not? Why do we have this inner drive to defy authority and cross that line? Why is there this pull to get back at someone when we are offended? It is because this is our nature.

Scripture testifies man has a sinful nature. While the witness of man's works provides ample evidence of his sinful nature, the scriptures forever settles the matter for it is the testimony of God Himself.

In his letter to the Ephesians, Paul characterized what his life and those of fellow Christians was like before they were converted.

> *You were dead in your trespasses and sins in which you formerly walked according to the course of this world, according to the prince of the power of the air, of the spirit that is now working in the sons of disobedience. Among them we too all formerly lived in the lusts of our flesh, indulging the desires of the flesh and of the mind, and were <u>by nature</u> children of wrath, even as the rest.* EPHESIANS 2:1-3

This is man's natural state prior to salvation. He "walked" or ordered his life in ways that conformed to Satan. He lived in his lusts and indulged himself. And this was his nature.

David confirmed his own sinful nature when he said:

> *Behold, I was brought forth in iniquity, And in sin my mother conceived me.* PSALM 51:5

David was not stating the sexual act between his parents was sinful. Rather he perceived his evil tendencies were part of his nature from his very conception.

Jesus confirmed man is evil despite his displays of kindness to his own children.

> *Or what man is there among you who, when his son asks for a loaf, will give him a stone? Or if he asks for a fish, he will not give him a snake, will he? If you then, <u>being evil</u>, know how to give good gifts to your children, how much more will your Father who is in heaven give what is good to those who ask Him!*
> MATTHEW 7:9–11

Jesus' point was that man, who is evil by nature, still responds kindly when requests are made by his children. That being the case, how much more will God, who has no such nature, be gracious to those who make requests of Him.

From the testimony of both human experience and scripture, mankind has a two-fold problem. He is not only guilty of countless sinful deeds. He is also at the very core of his being disposed towards sinful behavior. Yes, his sinful tendencies can be restrained through certain coercive measures. But even then the prevailing tendency in his heart is towards evil; that is why he must continue to be restrained.

Man not only needs to be forgiven; he needs to be inwardly transformed. Even if God somehow miraculously wiped away and forgave all a man's sins at a given point in time, it would not matter. That man would be guilty of countless other sins from that day forward, and store up for himself judgment again. Man is therefore destined to perish because of this dual reality.

> **Mankind has a two-fold problem. He has committed innumerable evil deeds which make him liable to God's judgment. He also has a heart which is bent on disobeying God's laws and defying authority. Man therefore not only needs to be forgiven. He also needs the innermost part of his being supernaturally transformed to be disposed towards righteousness, goodness, purity and love.**

Chapter 20

The Earthly Lives of Those Sentenced to Hell

Those sentenced to hell rejected the message of John 3:16, and as a result continued to live sinful lives.

Does scripture describe the earthly lives of those who are sentenced to hell? Is it clear what they were like in this world? Were there certain attitudes, activities, behaviors and beliefs that characterized them? The answer to these questions is a definite "Yes," and it is best understood in the profound statement of our Lord Jesus Himself, "You will know them by their fruits" (MATTHEW 7:16).

Scripture clearly teaches the identifying marks of those who are sentenced to hell. They are people who rejected the good news of Jesus Christ. And because of their rejection, God never endowed them with a righteous, godly disposition. They lived sinful lives. They may have been outwardly religious but were inwardly lawless. They hated God and persecuted His people. They never knew the true God. Examining each of these traits will give a clear profile of those sentenced to hell.

The Judgment God Desires to Withhold

People in hell rejected the good news of Jesus Christ. We have already established God's verdict is *no one* is righteous; *not even one*. And mankind has a two-fold problem: he owes God an insurmountable debt, and he has a sinful nature. But the good news is:

> *For God so loved the world, that He gave His only begotten Son, that <u>whoever believes in Him</u> shall not perish, but have eternal life.* JOHN 3:16

There is a condition to "not perish" and "have eternal life." It is to "believe in Him," Jesus Christ, the Son of God. But those in hell rejected this message. They

> <u>do not obey</u> *the gospel of our Lord Jesus.*
> 2 THESSALONIANS 1:8
>
> <u>*did not believe the truth*</u> 2 THESSALONIANS 2:12
>
> <u>*do not obey*</u> *the gospel of God* 1 PETER 4:17

Note these verses portray rejecting the gospel a moral issue of the heart involving disobedience.

Jesus said:

> *He who believes in the Son has eternal life; but he who <u>does not obey</u> the Son will not see life, but the <u>wrath of God abides on him</u>.* JOHN 3:36

This is the natural state of man: the wrath of God *hovers over him*. The wicked rejected God's gracious invitation to obey and believe, so the wrath that hovered over them was ultimately fulfilled in their being sentenced to hell.

In this series GOOD NEWS IN JOHN 3:16, what "believing in Him [Jesus]" means will be thoroughly explored in book 6, THE FAITH GOD REQUIRES TO SAVE. For now, what is critical to understand is people in hell rejected the gospel, and that rejection had a very serious consequence.

People in hell were never graciously endowed with a righteous, godly disposition. They remained in the fallen, sinful state they were born. God's Law was never inscribed on their heart; they never received God's life. This is substantially different from those whom God graciously transformed the moment they believed.

When a person believes in Jesus Christ, they are supernaturally and miraculously transformed at the core of their being. This is a gracious act of almighty God. Their old, sinful nature, which was disposed to sin and unrighteousness, dies. And the believer instantaneously receives a new nature; one disposed towards truth and righteousness. As such, they change. They still experience temptation, and fail in their Christian walk from time to time. But they get up, much like a toddler learning to walk. The life of a believer is characterized by purity and goodness, not by sin and evil.

Having a righteous, godly disposition does not mean a believer is perfect. Scripture presupposes genuine Christians will fall and need to be restored (GALATIANS 6:1). And the apostle John wrote "If we say that we have no sin, we are deceiving ourselves and the truth is not in us" (1 JOHN 1:8). Continued cleansing from sin is necessary even for believers, and that is why they are assured if they confess their sins they will be forgiven (1 JOHN 1:9). And scripture records the failures of many godly men, such as the apostle Peter's hypocrisy (GALATIANS 2:11-14). So the existence of isolated acts of sin in no way contradicts being a godly person — godly men fail.

But the existence of sin in a genuine believer must not be pressed too far. Having a righteous, godly disposition means a man's life is overall characterized by godliness. Yes, he still experiences temptation to do wrong and periodically yields to those temptations. But when he does he is grieved with a godly grief. He *hates* that he is tempted. And he does not live a life of indifference towards sin, and he most certainly does not celebrate it. A lifestyle of sin is utterly contrary to his new nature.

In this series GOOD NEWS IN JOHN 3:16, this inner transformation will be thoroughly explored in book 3, THE BLESSING GOD DESIRES TO BESTOW. For now, what is critical to understand is those who rejected the gospel never underwent a divine transformation of heart, so they retained their sinful nature. The consequence of this is clear.

People in hell lived sinful lives. Sexual immorality, impatience, selfishness, unrighteous anger and the like characterized them. Like all fallen men who are unconverted, they not only engaged in sinful activities, they enjoyed doing so. They

> *loved darkness rather than the Light, for their deeds were evil.* JOHN 3:19
>
> *took pleasure in wickedness.* 2 THESSALONIANS 2:12

This love of sin is the basis of numerous warnings regarding those who "do not inherit the kingdom of God."

> *Now the deeds of the flesh are evident, which are: immorality, impurity, sensuality, idolatry, sorcery, enmities, strife, jealousy, outbursts of anger, disputes, dissensions, factions, envying, drunkenness, carousing, and things like these, of which I forewarn you, just as I have forewarned you, that <u>those who practice</u>*

> *such things will not inherit the kingdom of God.*
> GALATIANS 5:19–21
>
> *Or do you not know that the unrighteous <u>will not inherit the kingdom of God</u>? Do not be deceived; neither fornicators, nor idolaters, nor adulterers, nor effeminate, nor homosexuals, nor thieves, nor the covetous, nor drunkards, nor revilers, nor swindlers, will inherit the kingdom of God.* 1 CORINTHIANS 6:9–10

These statements from the apostle Paul must be properly interpreted. He is not saying when a genuine Christian commits one of these acts, he forfeits the kingdom of God unless he confesses that sin immediately. Nor is he saying a genuine Christian will never under any circumstances commit one of these acts — godly men fail. Instead these verses portray what those who have not been saved and inwardly transformed are outwardly like. They have a casual, approving or celebratory attitude towards sin, and as such it is the general character of their lives.

People in hell rejected the very means God appointed for their own deliverance from sinful, degrading passions. It is not that fornicators, idolaters, adulterers, effeminate, homosexuals, thieves, the covetous, drunkards, revilers, and swindlers are beyond God's forgiveness. Indeed the churches in the New Testament were comprised of people who were delivered from such lifestyles — "such were some of you" (1 CORINTHIANS 6:9–10). The difference is those in hell refused to believe in Jesus Christ. As a result, they were never inwardly transformed by God into people who found such practices abhorrent, so they continued in them.

There is more than one reason why sinners loved their sin. Perhaps in their deceived, corrupted mind they did not view it as sin, and that is why they enjoyed it. Or maybe they knew it was sin and worthy of God's judgment, but they not only delighted in it but also gave "hearty approval" to those who did the same thing (ROMANS 1:29-32). Whatever the case, in their earthly life they *loved* sinning.

Oh how depraved are the hearts of men; they find pleasure in evil! People look *forward* to getting drunk. Drug addicts *anticipate* getting high. Thieves take *pride* in their plunder. Immoral people take *pleasure* in pornography, adultery, fornication, premarital sex, homosexuality and lesbianism. Legislators are *proud* to pass laws legalizing the murder of the unborn. Politicians *gleefully support* redefining marriage as something other than a union between a man and a woman. Men *unashamedly* dress and adorn themselves like women. Gang members find *excitement* in their thuggery. Supervisors find it *satisfying* to lord over their subordinates. Workers find *gratification* in shirking their job responsibilities. And the list goes on and on.

A sinful lifestyle is a lawless lifestyle; it is one that is not constrained at the heart level by God's Law. This is the character of those sentenced to hell: they were lawless.

> *Everyone who practices sin also practices lawlessness; and sin is lawlessness ...No one who abides in Him [Jesus Christ] sins ... Make sure no one deceives you; the one who practices righteousness is righteous, just as He is righteous; the one who practices sin is of the devil ... No one who is born of God practices sin ... By this the children of God and the children of the devil are obvious: anyone who does not practice righteousness is not of God, nor the one who does not love his brother.* 1 JOHN 3:4-10

The Earthly Lives of Those Sentenced to Hell

People in hell were not loving, merciful or compassionate. Whether it be holding a grudge, refusing to forgive, getting back at someone, calling a person a name, or the like, during their earthly lives people in hell were unkind, unmerciful people. This is the fallen nature of all unconverted men.

When a person believes in Jesus Christ, they undergo a supernatural transformation of being; the divine life of God indwells them. But God is by nature loving, kind, and gracious, so that is what believers become. In fact, scripture teaches love is the identifying mark of a genuine Christian, and anyone who is not a loving person is not a believer.

> *Beloved, let us love one another, for love is from God; and everyone who loves is born of God and knows God. <u>The one who does not love does not know God, for God is love.</u>* 1 JOHN 4:7–8

But unbelievers never underwent this divine transformation, so they remained in their fallen state.

Jesus taught a time would come where He Himself would pronounce judgment against merciless sinners.

> *Depart from Me, accursed ones, into the eternal fire … for I was hungry, and <u>you gave Me nothing</u> to eat; I was thirsty, and <u>you gave Me nothing</u> to drink; I was a stranger, and <u>you did not invite Me</u> in; naked, and <u>you did not clothe Me</u>; sick, and in prison, and <u>you did not visit Me</u>.* MATTHEW 25:42-43

This passage is not suggesting people enter heaven by engaging in good works. It is showing those who are accursed have never been inwardly and supernaturally transformed by God into compassionate people, especially towards believers. They have retained their fallen nature of being unloving, which is the basic nature of man.

In Jesus' parable of Lazarus and the wicked rich man condemned to hell, the rich man was just as uncompassionate. He dressed and dined extravagantly, neglecting poor Lazarus who struggled to even get a crumb from the rich man's table (LUKE 16:19–21). Jesus' teaching is clear: people in hell were not merciful people in their earthly lives. They were absorbed with their own luxuries, comforts, and pleasures. They were "lovers of pleasure rather than lovers of God" (2 TIMOTHY 3:4).

People in hell may have been outwardly religious but were inwardly lawless. There are countless people in every country that claim to know the true God through Jesus Christ. These people attend church, have been baptized, participate in the Lord's Supper, use Christian lingo, help the poor, assist in ministry outreaches, and provide financial support. But their Christianity is not genuine because they have a persistent casual or even celebratory attitude towards sin.

Jesus said in the judgment many outwardly religious people will be judged.

> *Many will say to Me on that day, "Lord, Lord, did we not prophesy in Your name, and in Your name cast out demons, and in Your name perform many miracles?" And then I will declare to them, "I never knew you; depart from me, you who practice lawlessness."*
> MATTHEW 7:22-23

Outward acts such as prophesying, casting out demons, and performing miracles can be inauthentic. Such a person may be self-deceived and living in sin, thinking they actually performed a miracle when in reality they did not. Or they may be consciously aware they do not have the ability to perform a miracle, but act as if they can for the sake of gaining popularity, money, or the like. Whatever the case, these people are condemned because they practiced lawlessness — their heart was not constrained by God's Law, and His commandments were not written on their hearts.

In Jesus earthly ministry He made a similar charge against the religious teachers of His day: the scribes and Pharisees.

> *Do not do according to their [the scribes and Pharisees] deeds; for <u>they say things and do not do them</u>. They tie up heavy burdens and lay them on men's shoulders, but they themselves are unwilling to move them with so much as a finger. But <u>they do all their deeds to be noticed by men</u>.* MATTHEW 23:1-5

Jesus then directly rebuked them for their hypocrisy.

> *But woe to you, scribes and Pharisees, hypocrites, because you shut off the kingdom of heaven from people; for you do not enter in yourselves ... you devour widows' houses, and for a pretense you make long prayers ... you have neglected the weightier provisions of the law: justice and mercy and faithfulness ... you clean the outside of the cup and of the dish, but inside they are full of robbery and self-indulgence ... you are like whitewashed tombs which on the outside appear beautiful, but inside they are full of dead men's bones and all uncleanness. So you, too, outwardly appear righteous to men, but inwardly you are full of hypocrisy and lawlessness ... You serpents, you brood of vipers, how will you escape the sentence of hell?* MATTHEW 23:13-33

The Judgment God Desires to Withhold

The scribes and Pharisees were highly respected and deemed godly examples. Indeed, they regarded themselves as righteous men who pleased God. But in reality they were hypocrites; a bunch of snakes who only served themselves and were destined for hell.

Judas is another example of someone who outwardly appeared righteous but was actually wicked. When a woman anointed Jesus with costly perfume, Judas asked why the perfume was not sold and given to the poor. But his question had an ulterior motive. "He said this, not because he was concerned about the poor, but because he was a thief, and as he had the money box, he used to pilfer what was put into it" (JOHN 12:5–6).

Scripture repeatedly warns of those who claim to speak for God, but are deceivers. These false teachers and false prophets may be smooth, eloquent speakers with friendly, charismatic personalities, but they are characterized by evil works.

> *[They] indulged in gross immorality* JUDE 1:7

> *[They] are caring only for themselves* JUDE 1:12

> *In their greed they exploit you with false words.* 2 PETER 2:3

> *These are grumblers, finding fault, following after their own lusts; they speak arrogantly, flattering people for the sake of gaining an advantage.* JUDE 1:16

> *[They are] reviling where they have no knowledge ... They count it a pleasure to revel in the daytime ... having eyes full of adultery that never cease from sin, enticing unstable souls, having a heart trained in greed.* 2 PETER 2:13-14

Despite their pretenses of being holy, they were never delivered from the greedy, lustful, selfish nature with which they were born. There was manipulation, intimidation, and deceitfulness, all with a view to satisfy their own insatiable desires for more.

People in hell hated God. They wanted nothing to do with Him. They despised Him, and thought evil of Him. This hatred is revealed through their hatred of Jesus Himself and His followers.

During Jesus earthly ministry He said to His disciples:

> *[The world] hates Me because I testify of it, that its deeds are evil.* JOHN 7:7

If Jesus' ministry consisted of talking about either Himself or sin in a way that was palatable to the world, He would not be hated. But Jesus, both in word and deed, testified He alone was the only way to God, and He likewise exposed the hypocrisy and unrighteousness of all men. Self-righteous people do not like being told they are sinners. And when they object and insist they are children of God, and are instead told they are children of the devil, it is not taken very well (JOHN 8:12-59). As a result, the world hated Him.

But hatred of Jesus should not be considered distinct from hatred of God. Jesus said:

> *He who hates Me hates My Father [God] also.*
> JOHN 15:23

If people had a problem with Jesus' message, actions or character, their issue was ultimately with God. But Jesus warned this same hatred would be directed at His disciples who kept Jesus' words and followed Him.

The Judgment God Desires to Withhold

> *If the world hates you, <u>you know that it has hated Me before it hated you</u>. If you were of the world, the world would love its own; but because you are not of the world, but I chose you out of the world, because of this the world hates you.* JOHN 15:18–19

So the world hated Jesus while He was on earth, and that hatred was actually a hatred of God. And Christ' followers, whose lives and message reflect that of Jesus, would likewise be hated. But how does this hatred manifest itself?

People in hell persecuted genuine Christians. Jesus was mocked, ridiculed, scoffed, derided, insulted, falsely accused, and ultimately murdered. And the same types of things happened to His apostles and disciples.

A genuine Christian understands he has nothing to commend himself to God, and salvation is a free gift. And he has been granted a new righteous, godly disposition, and as such does not have a casual or celebratory attitude towards sinning. This does not mean he walks around condemning everyone. It just means he does not embrace the godless values and lifestyles of the world. Whether it be crude humor, gossip, gluttony, premarital sex, same sex relationships, cross-dressing, or acceptance of the notion a person can actually change their own sex — the genuine Christian does not yield to these worldly currents. As a result, "they are surprised that you do not run with them into the same excesses of dissipation, and they *malign you*" (1 PETER 4:4).

Persecution has persisted from the time of Christ to the present day in varying ways and degrees. On the milder side, it manifests itself in the sentiment believers are misguided, undiscerning, or going through some sort of phase. In other cases there is disdain that manifests itself in a mocking gesture or scoffing remark. Other people deny privileges or sue Christians for issues related to their faith. And of course there are those who are openly hostile and physically abusive. In whatever form, persecution is something believers should expect since their inward transformation translates into their not embracing the views and practices of this fallen world.

> *All who desire to live godly in Christ Jesus <u>will be persecuted</u>.* 2 TIMOTHY 3:12

Of course there are those who embrace sinful lifestyles and profess to believe in Christ. There are independent churches and entire denominations that fall into this category. Such people are generally not persecuted by the world because they have adopted the world's standards. But by approving or embracing sinful practices, they show they are part of the world, and do not have the life of God within them.

People in hell were among those who in their earthly lives persecuted Christians. But their hatred of them was ultimately hatred against Jesus Christ and God the Father, even as the risen Lord Jesus told Saul: "Saul, Saul, why are you persecuting *Me*" (ACTS 9:4).

People in hell never knew the true God at any time. Even the devil and his fallen angels are aware of God's existence, and they know God in a distant, impersonal, intellectual way. But it is quite different to know God personally — to have an intimate, loving relationship with Him. People in hell *never* knew God this way while they lived on earth.

Jesus warned His disciples they would be persecuted by those who did not know God. He said:

> *If they persecuted Me, they will also persecute you ... But all these things they will do to you ... because <u>they do not know the One who sent Me</u>.* JOHN 15:20–21

It was this same lack of knowing God that contributed to the persecution of the Thessalonian Christians. Paul said of their persecutors:

> *It is only just for God to repay [your persecutors] with affliction ... <u>those who do not know God</u>.*
> 2 THESSALONIANS 1:6–8

And Jesus Himself declared in the judgment many outwardly religious people will be condemned.

> *I will declare to them, "<u>I never knew you</u>; depart from Me, you who practice lawlessness."* MATTHEW 6:23

In this pronouncement it is not that those whom Jesus condemns truly knew God at a certain time in their lives. It is not that they knew God, backslid, and remained in their backslid state. On the contrary, their character was consistent over the course of their life — consistently bad. They *never* knew Jesus Christ, and He *never* knew them. "I *never* knew you — *ever*."

> **People who are sentenced to hell rejected the gospel. As a result, they remained in their fallen, corrupted state. They never possessed a righteous, godly disposition. They lived sinful lives, and were uncompassionate people. They may have been outwardly religious, but inwardly they were lawless. They hated God and persecuted His people. They never knew God at any time in their lives.**

CHAPTER 21

The Attitude of those in Hell

Those in hell hate God, love sin, and are completely and utterly intransigent as respects evil.

What is the attitude of those who face God's judgment and are sentenced to hell? We know what they were like on earth, but what about when they finally stand before God and are judged? When they are subject to fiery torment, darkness and the absence of all God's mercies, we know they are in great mental anguish. They weep and are in agony. But how do they respond while undergoing their suffering?

Some think people in hell are truly repentant, crying out for forgiveness only to have God sternly reply "It is too late! You had your chance while on earth! Now you must suffer your judgment!" But this conception is far removed from the biblical portrayal of hell. Several observations can be made.

Hell's captives never have a broken and contrite spirit. This is evident because of God's unchanging nature. David said:

> *The sacrifices of God are a broken spirit; A broken and a contrite heart, O God, You will not despise.*
> PSALM 51:17

God eternally delights in showing mercy, and He takes "no pleasure in the death of the wicked" (EZEKIEL 33:11). But those in hell are *never* of a broken spirit.

No doubt people in hell are weeping and experiencing mental anguish, but they are sorrowful for the wrong reason. They only possess a self-centered sorrow, not a godly sorrow. These two radically different types of sorrow are clearly seen in Cain and David.

When God pronounced judgment on Cain for murdering his brother Abel, Cain's response was a self-centered sorrow. "My punishment is too great to bear … I will be a vagrant and a wanderer on the earth, and whoever finds me will kill me" (GENESIS 4:13-14). Cain's response would be similar to a murderer responding to a life prison sentence with "This penalty is too great! I had so many plans in life. What will happen to me in prison!" Such a response shows the guilty party is only sorrowful for himself and what he has to suffer. But there is no consciousness of the vileness of his deed before God combined with a humble appeal for God's gracious pardon.

Contrast Cain's response with that of David who had committed adultery with Bathsheba and had her husband murdered. How did David respond to God? He said "Be gracious to me, O God, according to your lovingkindness … blot out my transgressions … wash me thoroughly from my iniquity … Against You, You only, I have sinned and done what is evil in Your sight … Create in me a clean heart …" (PSALM 51). David's response is a broken and contrite heart, and reflects godly sorrow.

Hell's captives never have a heart attitude like David. They are never crushed before God by the weight of their own sins and humbly ask for His gracious pardon. They *never* do this.

Hell's captives are absolutely intransigent of their evil works. It is not if they had opportunity they would cease being covetous, malicious, or lustful. The evil heart they had in their earthly life is the same heart they possess in hell.

The book of Revelation is a prophecy of God's judgment of this evil world. In that day God brings numerous plagues on the earth. But fallen men do not repent no matter what fierce judgments God brings.

> *A third of mankind was killed by these three plagues, by the fire and the smoke and the brimstone ... The rest of mankind ... did not repent of the works of their hands, so as not to worship demons, and the idols of gold and of silver and of brass and of stone and of wood, which can neither see nor hear nor walk; and they did not repent of their murders nor of their sorceries nor of their immorality nor of their thefts.* REVELATION 9:18-21

> *Men were scorched with fierce heat; and they blasphemed the name of God who has the power over these plagues, and they did not repent so as to give Him glory ... the beast, and his kingdom became darkened; and they gnawed their tongues because of pain, and they blasphemed the God of heaven because of their pains and their sores; and they did not repent of their deeds.* REVELATION 16:9-11

The attitude of sinners judged while on earth in the day of judgment continues into their eternal punishment. In hell even though they know they are being subject to fiery torment and darkness for their unrighteous deeds, they are absolutely unrepentant.

The Judgment God Desires to Withhold

Hell's captives are enraged at God. We know during their earthly lives unbelievers hated God and persecuted His people. And in the day of judgment they "blaspheme God because of their pains and their sores" (REVELATION 16:11). There is no reason to think hell's torments has any different effect on them. Their unfulfilled rage is likely part of their torment.

Seven times Jesus associated hell as a place where there is "weeping and gnashing of teeth." Weeping obviously signifies pain and suffering. But the phrase "gnashing of teeth" may reflect the intensity of anguish, the anger at the righteous, or both. The phrase is frequently used in Psalms to describe the hatred of the wicked against the righteous, such as Psalm 37:12 which says "The wicked plots against the righteous And gnashes at him with his teeth." And when Stephen preached and charged the leaders with resisting the Holy Spirit, they were likewise exceedingly angry and gnashed at him with their teeth (ACTS 7:54).

When the wicked stand before the Lord and are made aware they are not entering the kingdom, they object and say "Lord, Lord, did we not prophesy ... cast out demons, and in Your name perform many miracles?" (MATTHEW 7:21). In their response we can detect both bewilderment and annoyance — they are not posing a submissive inquiry with a view to accept the Lord's judgments. What they are saying is, "Lord, Lord, certainly You do not mean *we* are excluded from Your kingdom. You most assuredly must be mistaken. *We* performed miracles! *We* cast out demons! How could you regard *us* as unworthy!" They are perplexed and confused over their rejection, and it arouses their indignation. And when He says "Depart from Me, you who practice lawlessness," is there any reason to think they will accept His verdict? Will they become docile, submissive and have a change of heart?

Hell's captives have the same character as the devil and his fallen angels. Scripture describes the devil as a murderer, adversary, enemy, tempter, liar, robber, and accuser. He is conniving, deceitful, cruel, merciless, remorseless, brutal, and hateful. But Jesus and His apostles frequently classified those who were hostile to God as the devil's children. Jesus said

> *You are seeking to kill Me, a man who has told you the truth, which I heard from God … <u>You are of your father the devil, and you want to do the desires of your father.</u>* JOHN 8:40–44

And in the final judgment, Jesus tells the wicked:

> *Depart from Me, accursed ones, into the eternal fire <u>which has been prepared for the devil and his angels.</u>* MATTHEW 25:41

Sinful man goes to the same place the devil and his fallen angels go because they are of the same character and nature.

Every person born into this world is by nature at enmity with God and rebellious. In this sense, all mankind resembles the devil. Those in hell never believed, so they never underwent the supernatural transformation by God to make them disposed towards righteousness. They never became children of God, but remained children of the devil.

> **Even when those sentenced to hell experience the full brunt of God's wrath and are subject to great suffering, they do not have a broken and contrite spirit. They do not repent of their evil deeds. They remain angry at God, and hate Him. In doing so they aligned themselves with Satan in his rebellion against God.**

Chapter 22

Paul's Treatise on Man's Condemnation

"There is none righteous, no, not even one."

John 3:16 is the good news or "gospel" of God in a very condensed form, concisely expressing God's desire to save mankind from judgment. All the apostles of Jesus Christ were divinely commissioned to convey this message of hope to the world. While John 3:16 is among the most succinct expressions of the gospel, the apostle Paul's letter to the Romans is among the most detailed, systematic treatments of it.

In the greeting at the beginning of the letter, Paul emphasizes his divinely appointed role as one to whom the gospel was entrusted. He expresses he was "set apart for the gospel of God," that he "served God in the preaching of the gospel," that he was "eager to preach the gospel to you also who are in Rome," and that He was "not ashamed of the gospel, for it is the power of God to salvation" (ROMANS 1:1-17).

After confirming his commission as God's appointed custodian of the gospel, Paul embarks on delineating its actual content in the rest of the letter. But in doing so, the *first thing* Paul teaches is the universal condemnation of mankind. This spans from Romans 1:18 – 3:20, and comprises 15% of the entire letter. His goal is to prove that God, in the examination of man's works, has determined *all* are sinners and worthy of judgment; there are *no exceptions*. Paul makes his case by breaking all humanity into three distinct categories: devout religious Jews, ethical people (whether Jews or Gentiles) who condemned sinful practices, and idolatrous immoral Gentiles who gleefully sinned. In this way he covers the entire moral spectrum.

On the one end you have devout, religious Jews. The Jews were God's chosen people, descendants of Abraham to whom God promised to make a great nation. God Himself would rule that nation, and through it all the other nations of the world would be blessed. God Himself commanded Abraham and all his descendants to observe the rite of circumcision as a sign of God's covenant blessings. Abraham was the father of Isaac, and Isaac was the father of Jacob. And God Himself gave Jacob the name "Israel."

Over hundreds of years the children of Israel became a great nation in accordance with God's promise. God Himself gave the nation His moral Law, the Ten Commandments, miraculously engraved on stone. The religious rite of circumcision and the centrality of God's Law formed Israel's national identity, and it is what separated them from other nations throughout history. The Jews deemed themselves secure from God's judgment on account of having been circumcised and given God's Law.

On the other end you have idolatrous Gentiles. The Gentiles were those who were not Israelites or Jews. As such, they also were not recipients of God's covenant promises. The nations to which they belonged did not have God's Law or genuine prophets to convey God's infallible messages. Gentiles were given to the worship of false gods through idols. And as a society they were unashamedly engaged in gross debauchery. Murder, rioting, cruelty, sexual perversions, rebellion and the like were things they not only openly engaged in, but were proud of.

In-between the devout, religious Jews and the immoral, idolatrous Gentiles, you have ethical people who condemned evil practices. These could be Jews or Gentiles who did not approve of the murderous, sexually immoral, rebellious behaviors of others. They not only recognized such behaviors were morally wrong. They strove to do the right thing and condemned those who brazenly sinned.

From these three categories, the contrast cannot be more stark. The Jews are enlightened as to who is the true God, circumcised as a covenant rite to that God, knowledgeable of His commands as revealed in His Law, and part of a nation and culture that reinforced the Law through parental instruction, national festivals, and weekly religious assemblies. The idolatrous Gentiles are unenlightened, uncircumcised, ignorant of God's Law, worshipers of false gods through idolatry, and are sexually immoral, violent, and totally depraved. The ethical people include anyone who strove to do the right thing and condemn the depraved activities of others.

Paul systematically shows all three categories of people are liable to God's judgment. His points may be restated this way:

1. Idolatrous, immoral Gentiles are liable to God's judgment because they sin having rejected God's revelation of Himself in creation.

2. Ethical people (whether Jew or Gentile) who condemn the sinful behavior of others are liable to God's judgment because they also sin like those whom they condemn.

3. Religious Jews are liable to God's judgment because they sin despite having God's Law and being circumcised.

This division of thought is clearly seen in Paul's use of words and general themes.

In the first section, Romans 1:18-32, we clearly see Paul has idolatrous, immoral Gentiles in view. He continually employs "them" and "they" throughout this section; a marked contrast from the use of "you" and "your" in the other sections. "*They* are without excuse," "*they* did not honor him as God," "*they* became fools" and so on. Paul also specifically cites idolatry as the trait of these people. They "exchanged the glory of the incorruptible God for an *image*" and they "served the *creature* rather than the creator." Finally, he strongly condemns their character in relation to sin. They are "filled with all unrighteousness, wickedness, greed, evil; full of envy, murder, strife, deceit, malice; they are gossips, slanderers, haters of God, insolent, arrogant, boastful, inventors of evil, disobedient to parents, without understanding, untrustworthy, unloving, unmerciful; and *although they know the ordinance of God, that those who practice such things are worthy of death, they not only do the same, but also give hearty approval to those who practice them.*" These idolatrous, immoral Gentiles are portrayed as the worst for they enjoy sinning.

Paul argues idolatrous Gentiles are liable to God's judgment because they sin having rejected God's revelation of Himself in creation. Gentiles did not have the benefit of the revelation of God's Law like the Jews. But Gentiles did have another revelation that has existed throughout human history: the testimony of God's existence, power and divine nature as manifested in creation. But rather than worship God as a holy, all-powerful Being separate from His creation, they "became futile in their speculations" and "exchanged the glory of the incorruptible God for an image in the form of corruptible man and of birds and four-footed animals and crawling creatures" — their gods were idols in the image of man, animals or insects. What should have been self-evident in observing nature — God's transcendent existence — they rejected. From there they rejected other things that should also have been evident from nature: that men and women were sexually designed for each other. But they rejected this obvious lesson from nature also, and instead engaged in homosexuality and lesbianism. Three times Paul uses the phrase "God gave them over" to signify God's permitting fallen men to fulfill their evil, sexually perverse desires and engage in all manner of wickedness. Since these Gentiles rejected the revelation of God in creation, they are liable to God's judgment.

In the second section, Romans 2:1-16, Paul has in view ethical people who condemn those who gleefully engage in evil behaviors like those just cited. Here Paul uses "you" and "your" as opposed to "they" and "them." "*You* are storing up wrath for yourself," "do *you* think lightly," "because of *your* stubbornness," and so on. He also begins this section by specifically citing the character of those in view as those who judge, repeating himself three times. "Therefore you have no excuse, everyone of *you who passes judgment*, for in that which *you judge another*, you condemn yourself; for *you who judge* practice the same things." Paul has in mind ethical people who view themselves as morally superior to others because they do not unashamedly and gleefully engage in sinful behavior.

Paul argues ethical people who condemn others are liable to God's judgment because they still sin themselves. They may not gleefully practice sinning like others, but that is not the point. God's judgment is based on whether you *sinned*, not whether you *gleefully* sinned and are *happy about it*. To put it another way, the issue is not whether you nod your head in agreement with God and say, "It is *wrong* to do this or that." The issue is whether you *do this or that*. Since even ethical people fall short of this standard, they are liable to God's judgment as well.

In the third section, Romans 2:17-29, Paul specifically has Jews in view. He begins this section with the phrase "But if *you* bear the name '*Jew*'" and describes them as those who have been "instructed out of the Law." He then goes on to completely dismantle the two things every Jew thought safeguarded them from God's judgment: the Law and the rite of circumcision.

Paul argues Jews are liable to God's judgment because they still sin despite having God's Law and being circumcised. Yes, they may have received the revelation of God's Law and agree it is good not to steal or commit adultery — but they still steal and commit adultery. And as respects circumcision, what value is being circumcised if the person breaks God's holy Law? Sinning essentially negates one's circumcision. So Jews are also sinners, and liable to God's judgment as well.

In the fourth and final section on man's universal condemnation, Romans 3:1-20, Paul summarizes everything he has established in the previous three sections. After a short digression on the value of a Jewish heritage, he quotes numerous scriptures stating the inescapable conclusion: "There is none righteous, not even one." This is God's verdict on all mankind whether it be the immoral idolater, ethical person or devout Jew. Everyone is without excuse, stands condemned before God, and is worthy of judgment.

Paul's treatise showing the just condemnation of these three different groups is far reaching. Several points are in order.

Man still rejects God's revelation of Himself in nature. He is just more sophisticated about it now. Scientists, philosophers and other highly educated people authoritatively declare "God does not exist," "Nothing in science requires the existence of a personal God," or "There is no personal God; there are only forces in nature that bring order to the universe." Such statements may seem profound, insightful and wise to the minds of fallen men. But in reality such pontifications only reveal the utter blindness of the speakers — they are all as guilty of rejecting God's self-revelation in creation (and as foolish) as the man who worships a tree.

Homosexuality and lesbianism are not only immoral but also unnatural. One does not even need to look at a Bible to reach this conclusion. Even a young child given a block puzzle knows the square block belongs with the square socket, and the triangular block belongs with the triangular one. But modern man has not only rejected the evidence in creation of a transcendent God. He has also rejected basic, rudimentary principles of what nature teaches regarding sexuality. Homosexuality and lesbianism involves sexually unnatural activity — simple observations of male and female anatomy should make this obvious.

While the world may consider these unnatural sexual expressions indications of moral progress, in reality they indicate a greater depth of depravity and blindness that God desires to save individuals from. When a society deems those who consider same sex relationships unnatural as being insensitive, hateful, or bigoted, it reveals not how radical are those who hold to a heterosexual view of sexual expression, but rather how completely blind to even natural reason society has become.

Paul's arguments apply to ethical people no matter where they are in the moral spectrum. It does not matter how distorted and twisted a person's standards may be. They stand condemned even on the basis of those standards.

No matter where people land on the moral scale, there always exists some behaviors they deem morally unacceptable. The faithful husband may regard the unmarried couple living together immoral. That couple may deem adultery immoral. The adulterer may deem lesbianism immoral. And lesbians may in turn deem prostitution wrong. Everyone has *something* they consider morally wrong.

Paul's argument of man's sinfulness applies to every person right where they are at. We could say "You who say you should not be sexually immoral, you also say it is wrong to lie. Have you ever been sexually immoral or lied? Never mind whether you were proud of it, *did you commit the act?* If you are going to judge other people for their wrongdoings based on your own standards of right and wrong, have you not violated your own standards countless times and thereby condemned yourself?"

Professing Christians can make the same error as Jews by thinking they are protected from God's judgment on the basis of works. Baptism, attending church, and giving thanks over meals are all things Jesus and His apostles taught. But doing these things in no way safeguards a person from God's judgment. And yet how many people adopt this false view! People think "I will be spared God's judgment; I have been baptized" or "God will not judge me; I go to church every Sunday." Is this not the same error the Jews made as respects circumcision?

Paul's arguments against this type of thinking could likewise be employed. We could say "If a man is not baptized and yet fulfills all the other commands of Christ, is he not for all practical purposes baptized? And if you are baptized, and yet you do not keep all Christ' commands, have you not negated your baptism?" The point is baptism, church attendance, and praying over meals in no way protects a person from God's judgment. Good works in no way saves a person.

> **Paul the apostle was divinely commissioned by God with the gospel or "good news." An essential part of the gospel is understanding all mankind is guilty of sin and worthy of God's judgment — this is true of Gentiles, ethical people, and religious Jews. Gentiles are liable to God's judgment because they sin having rejected God's self-revelation in creation as a transcendent, all-powerful God. Ethical people who denounce the immoral practices of others are liable to God's judgment because they violate their own standards of right and wrong. Religious Jews are liable to God's judgment because they still sin even though they have fulfilled religious rites and know God's Law. You fall into one or more of these three categories, and therefore you likewise are liable to God's judgment**

CHAPTER 23

The Stubbornness of Hell's Captives

Hell does not reflect God's cruelty but rather man's obstinacy.

The world deems the Christian doctrine of hell repulsive. To fallen men it makes God out to be cruel. They may object and say "Why would a loving God create a person whom He knew would ultimately end up in hell? It would show greater compassion to not even create such a person!"

Despite all the worldly objections, hell does not reflect God's cruelty but rather man's obstinacy. And such accusations only demonstrate man's deceived, hardened heart. God *is* loving, just, and gracious. It is *man* who is cruel, unjust, and hateful. Several remarks will clearly contrast God's benevolence against man's stubbornness.

Man put himself in the position of being liable to God's judgment. It is not that there is a subgroup within mankind that is innately good and whom God deems just and righteous, and everyone else is immoral and selfish and thereby considered corrupt and evil. On the contrary, *all* are unrighteous. *All* have sinned. And *man did this to himself.*

Hell is what man has *earned*. Man examines himself using human standards and also compares himself to other men. But God examines man using His holy Law and compares men to those righteous standards. And in doing so He considers each man's outward actions as well as his heart, thoughts, desires, intents, and conscience. The result is everyone is deserving of condemnation. The kind, gentle, and conscientious, as well as the impatient, rude and selfish stand condemned before God.

That man finds himself in the terrible predicament of being liable to God's judgment is *his own* doing. God merely pronounces sentence based on the evidence before Him. Man *put himself* in his situation by being a rebellious, disobedient scoundrel. Man has no basis to blame God for the threat of hell when man *put himself* in that position to begin with.

God takes no pleasure in condemning men to hell. He yearns for man to come into relationship with Himself, and be spared judgment.

> *The Lord ... is ... <u>not wishing for any to perish</u> but for all to come to repentance.* 2 PETER 3:9

And again.

> *<u>I take no pleasure in the death of the wicked,</u> but rather that the wicked turn from his way and live.* EZEKIEL 33:11

God takes no delight in seeing men suffer in hell. His desire is that all men be saved from judgment. It is *impossible* for God's heart to be otherwise, because God in His very nature is love. Grace, kindness, patience, long suffering, and mercy — this is who He is. His loving, gracious, kind nature is only overruled when His wisdom, justice, and righteousness demands it.

God has made provision so no one need be sentenced to hell. In this book series GOOD NEWS IN JOHN 3:16, this provision is the sacrifice of His Son, Jesus Christ, and will be fully explored in book 5: THE SAVING WORK OF JESUS CHRIST. What needs to be recognized here is no one needs to go to hell. That is what the good news of John 3:16 is all about. While man is worthy of condemnation, *He need not suffer that fate.*

God made this provision even though the entire world was in rebellion against Him.

> *For one will hardly die for a righteous man; though perhaps for the good man someone would dare even to die. But God demonstrates His own love toward us, in that <u>while we were yet sinners</u>, Christ died for us.* ROMANS 5:7–8

So God openly displayed His good will to all mankind. To we who are hateful, murderous, unkind, immoral, unthankful and deserving of wrath, God sent His Son to die on our behalf so we could be spared judgment. *No one* has to be sentenced to hell.

Hell's captives spurned all God's attempts to save them. It is not that God earnestly desired fallen man to be saved, made provision to that end, and then did not take it upon Himself to move man in that direction. On the contrary, He actively and passionately pursues fallen man, even when He knows they will reject Him.

God moves upon all men to be saved, and seeks to draw them to Himself. He does this through ordinary people who share His message of love to the world. When that message is shared, He supernaturally moves upon men's hearts through His Holy Spirit, and brings conviction.

The Judgment God Desires to Withhold

Stephen testified of God to the wicked religious leaders of his day. But he perceived while giving his message they were receiving none of it. He likely saw the scowls on their faces while giving his discourse. After giving a stirring message, he proclaimed:

> *You men who are stiff-necked and uncircumcised in heart and ears are <u>always resisting the Holy Spirit</u>; you are doing just as your fathers did.* ACTS 7:51

God was moving upon these religious leaders supernaturally through His Holy Spirit. But they were resisting Him as they had done many times before, fighting God's attempt to save them. They were stubborn and obstinate. To God's overtures of kindness and appeals to believe they became stiff-necked, hardened their hearts, stopped their ears, and closed their eyes. Their fierce hatred resulted in murdering Stephen; the very one God had sent to yet again draw them.

To end up in hell a man must vehemently fight God — *he must fight long and hard.*

God sends His word through His messengers time and time again to the lost. A man may stumble across a billboard, commercial, or broadcast where a preacher appeals to receive Jesus Christ. Or he may hear a conversion testimony from his parent, sibling, child or friend. Whatever the means, God sends His people to share His message that forgiveness and reconciliation is freely available. But those in hell rejected that message time and again, resisting the Holy Spirit. And there comes a point in God's wrestlings with man that He reluctantly, firmly and in wrath says, "*I will strive with you no longer! If this is the way you want it, then this is the way it will be!*"

Man is condemned to hell by his free choice. In one sense, people in hell receive the desire of their heart. They want nothing to do with God. They hate Him and everything He stands for. They just want God to leave them alone, and they fight all His attempts to draw them to Himself. So God reluctantly but in justice grants their request. They are forsaken by Him and cast into an isolated, miserable existence absent of all God's mercies.

All the angels were created in a *state of righteousness*; they were *naturally disposed* towards *goodness*, and did what was right. But angels were created free agents, and the choice God gave them was whether they wanted to *remain* in that righteous state, or *rebel*. A subgroup within them made the decision to rebel, Satan having initiated the rebellion. This decision of the fallen angels was their perpetual, free choice: they loved darkness rather than light.

In contrast man is born into this world in a *state of unrighteousness*; he is born *naturally disposed* towards *evil*, and does what is wrong. But men are created free agents, and the choice God gives man is whether he wants to *escape* his unrighteous state, or *continue* in rebellion. A subgroup within mankind makes the decision to receive the free gift of eternal life, God Himself having initiated their deliverance through Jesus Christ. The rest of mankind chooses to reject God. This decision of fallen man to remain in his unrighteous state is his perpetual, free choice: they too love darkness rather than light.

God is blameless in His dealings with man. It is not that God desires man to be condemned; God truly desires mankind to be saved. And God does not implant in man's heart the will to perpetually reject Him; that will arises from man's own heart. Nor does God withhold from man the grace necessary to receive Him; that grace is given, but man resists the Spirit's moving, and that resistance likewise arises solely from man's heart. Man's perpetual rejection of God originates solely from man himself.

God does not force any man to enter into a relationship with Himself — any relationship necessarily involves a free decision from both parties to associate. If men choose a solitary existence undergoing fiery torment rather than humbling themselves before God and enjoying eternal bliss, *that is their decision*. God made all the provisions necessary for them to avoid their miserable fate. *They* are the ones who choose defiance over obedience, self-will over humility, rebellion over submission, cursedness over blessedness, and torment over joy. *And they perpetually make this same choice — moment after moment, eon after eon.* Their hatred of God and love of sin, much like the fallen angels, reflects their *eternal character*.

> **The sentence of hell does not reveal God's cruelty but rather your obstinacy. You put yourself in the place of being liable to God's judgment. The threat of hell stems from God rightly assessing what you deserve for your works. God has no desire for you to perish in hell, and He made provision so you do not have to suffer your miserable fate. He pursues you and all men to save them from judgment, moving supernaturally on their hearts through His Holy Spirit in the preaching of the gospel. Those who are ultimately sentenced to hell have vehemently fought God's attempts to save them. And they freely, willfully, and perpetually choose hell over a relationship with God.**

CHAPTER 24

"Perish" as Used in John 3:16

For God so loved the world, that He gave His only begotten Son, that whoever believes in Him shall not perish, but have eternal life. JOHN 3:16

We are now ready to revisit John 3:16 and expand upon the word "perish." This word reflects the destiny of all mankind apart from God's intervention. The Christian teaching in view is that of God's judgment and hell.

For God so loved the world, that He gave His only begotten Son, that whoever believes in Him shall not suffer the punishment God Himself is obligated in justice to impose. God, in His perfect knowledge, has passed a verdict regarding the entire human race: there is no one who is righteous, not even one. Everyone is unjust, depraved, evil, and murderous. This verdict is based on God's judging according to His holy Law, the Ten Commandments. Man violates this Law both outwardly in his actions, and inwardly in his thoughts, desires, intents, and reasonings. In keeping with God's verdict and just character, He has determined every person is worthy to be sentenced to

> *fiery torment, darkness, and have all His gracious mercies withheld. But God does not want to impose this sentence. He does not want anyone to perish in hell, but instead have eternal life.* JOHN 3:16

To those who are open to the moving of God's Spirit, this book will birth a great appreciation and love for Jesus Christ. Like the story of the sinful woman who anointed Jesus' feet and washed them with her hair, we too understand the depths of sin we have been forgiven, and the terrible judgment we have been graciously spared.

But to those who have no interest in knowing the true God and His only begotten Son Jesus Christ, this book will be met with indifference, mockery, or indignation.

The testimony of scripture is sufficient to awaken one's mind to the truth of the gospel. Let each man choose as He will.

> *And he [the evil rich man in hell] said, "Then I beg you, father [Abraham], that you send him [Lazarus] to my father's house — for I have five brothers — in order that he may warn them, so that they will not also come to this place of torment." But Abraham said, "They have Moses and the Prophets; let them hear them." But he said, "No, father Abraham, but if someone goes to them from the dead, they will repent!" But he said to him, "<u>If they do not listen to Moses and the Prophets, they will not be persuaded even if someone rises from the dead.</u>"* LUKE 16:27–31

"Perish" as Used in John 3:16

THE JUDGMENT GOD DESIRES TO WITHHOLD

Suggested Reading

Blayney, B., Thomas Scott, and R.A. Torrey with Canne, John, Browne. *The Treasury of Scripture Knowledge*. London: Samuel Bagster and Sons, n.d.

Edwards, Jonathan. *The Works of Jonathan Edwards. Vol. 1.* Banner of Truth Trust, 1974.

Faithlife LLC, *Logos Bible Software*. Bellingham, WA

Jamieson, Robert, A. R. Fausset, and David Brown. *Commentary Critical and Explanatory on the Whole Bible*. Oak Harbor, WA: Logos Research Systems, Inc., 1997.

Malkin, Peter Z. and Harry Stein. *Eichmann in My Hands: A first-person account by the Israeli agent who captured Hitler's chief executioner.* New York: Open Road Integrated Media, 2018

Manser, Martin H. *Dictionary of Bible Themes: The Accessible and Comprehensive Tool for Topical Studies*. London: Martin Manser, 2009.

Visit Rushwave.org

*Establishing Believers
in the Christian Faith*

*This book is available as a paperback,
hardcover, e-book, audiobook, and video*

www.ingramcontent.com/pod-product-compliance
Lightning Source LLC
Chambersburg PA
CBHW060529080526
44586CB00012B/682